CAÑONERO II

CAÑONERO II

The RAGS TO RICHES STORY *of the*
KENTUCKY DERBY'S MOST IMPROBABLE WINNER

MILTON C. TOBY

THE
History
PRESS

Published by The History Press
Charleston, SC 29403
www.historypress.net

Copyright © 2014 by Milton C. Toby
All rights reserved

Front cover, bottom: Courtesy of Keeneland/*Thoroughbred Times*.

First published 2014

ISBN 978-1-5402-2167-4

Library of Congress CIP data applied for.

CONTENTS

FOREWORD

I t is a story that has been crying out to be told for over four decades, a story that no fiction writer could ever conceive.

It wasn't until I became a feature writer for the *Daily Racing Form* in 1991 that I embarked on the written journey of Cañonero II, a horse whose story amazed me in 1971 and still amazes me today. As I kept gathering additional pieces to this incredible story, new revised features appeared in the *DRF* and then the *Blood-Horse*, where I have been senior correspondent for the past fifteen years. I was determined not to let the story of Cañonero wither with the years.

With every word of this fairy tale came visions of a movie or a book, even in the form of an animated film or children's book. One of my constant goals as a writer has been to tell the fairy tale side of Thoroughbred racing, the stories that strip away our hardened exteriors and reach into the core of our soul to make the Sport of Kings a magical place that sustains its energy from the implausible truth.

As my revised stories on Cañonero continued to appear, eventually in my blog/column on Bloodhorse.com, there came constant requests to tell the story of Cañonero in a book. But having written six books for the *Blood-Horse*'s publishing arm, Eclipse Press, and serving as contributing writer on several others, I simply did not have the time to devote to a story that was so close to my heart and would require even more time and extensive research than I was able to give it.

Finally, two years ago, I was contacted by producer Salomon Gill, a native of Venezuela, who was intent on making a major motion picture about

Cañonero, based in good part on my writings, complete with an introductory documentary and a talented team of top actors and filmmakers. I was asked to be part of that team, as consultant and as an actual character in the movie. Needless to say, I was flattered and overjoyed to hear that the story of Cañonero was in such enthusiastic and skillful hands.

Then, recently, I was contacted by longtime racing writer Milt Toby, whose writings in *Blood-Horse* back in the 1970s when I was librarian for the *Daily Racing Form* and a fledgling freelance writer provided a good deal of my reading material. Milt had begun work on a Cañonero book, much to my delight. Having already done a brilliant job on the much darker story of Dancer's Image, Milt was the perfect person to embark on this monumental project. He had the experience of the times and the expertise to do the story justice. The Cañonero story finally was going to be told, in written form as well as visually. And most importantly, it was going to be told by talented artists who have been touched and inspired by this story as much as I have.

I thank Milt for doing all the dirty work and exhaustive research that I was unable or unwilling to take on. As a result, the Cañonero story has been told on these pages in great detail and with the passion it deserves. I also thank Milt for asking me to write the foreword, which has enabled me to grab a small hold of this comet as it reappears after so many years.

The story you are about to read is about a crooked-legged horse of obscure parents who was sold for a paltry $1,200 and arrived in Venezuela with a split hoof and a bad case of worms. Turned over to trainer Juan Arias, who had grown up in the slums of Caracas, this unlikeliest of heroes embarked on arguably the most amazing journey in the annals of Thoroughbred racing, beginning with its flight to the United States on a plane filled with chickens and ducks and continuing through its breathtaking victories in the Kentucky Derby and Preakness.

In between were a series of mini dramas that would come together to produce an epic tale of the turf that defied all logic and conventional thinking. There was nothing logical or conventional about Cañonero or his story, which included the owner's deceased mother appearing in a dream to foretell the story that is about to unfold, a crumpled cocktail napkin that could have altered the course of history and a number of uncommon ailments, none of which could stop this runaway express train until the final leg of the Triple Crown.

By then, the ugly duckling that was considered a mockery in the United States after arriving in Kentucky had become a national hero in both South and North America and the pride of Spanish-speaking people from both continents.

As I concluded in my latest story, when Cañonero died at Haras Tamanaco in 1981 after returning to Venezuela, the magnificent decade of the seventies was history, with Secretariat, Forego, Seattle Slew, Affirmed, Alydar and Spectacular Bid all stamping their place in the record books. But few remembered that it was Cañonero that paved the way for these media stars.

By the time of his death, the cries of "Viva Cañonero" had faded to a whisper, and the horse that had electrified the racing world, drawing the largest crowd in Belmont history, had slipped quietly back into the obscurity from which he came.

Cañonero's Derby and Preakness trophies were given to La Rinconada Racetrack, but they were never exhibited anywhere. The statue of him that had been commissioned was never built. As the years pass by and a new, younger core of high-tech racing fans emerge with little grasp of history, the name of Cañonero drifts deeper into memory, as do his amazing feats.

But after four decades, it is time to remember Cañonero and a special time in racing when the entire sport was set ablaze by a horse they called the "Caracas Cannonball."

You are now about to embark on this remarkable journey, thanks to Milt Toby and the passion and brilliant storytelling that exudes from every page.

Each chapter smolders with the tension and bigotry of the times, but also interjects the humor that accompanies all the odd-shaped pieces that make up this complex puzzle. When you come to the final gut-wrenching ending, before you will be a picture you will not soon forget.

By the end, you will be shouting "Viva Cañonero," and a new generation of Cañonero fans and admirers will be born. Sometimes, it takes talented people like Milt Toby and Salomon Gill to help move history up into the present and expose people to stories long forgotten.

STEVE HASKIN
Hamilton Square, New Jersey

PREFACE

Sometimes frustrating, sometimes exciting, research can be the most interesting part of the writing process. Without source material, however, there can be no meaningful research. Libraries and museums at Keeneland, Churchill Downs, Saratoga and a host of other locations do an excellent job at preservation, and their efforts must be applauded and supported. But what of the vast archives at racetracks and in private collections? Digitizing historic photographs and written material is a step in the right direction but is not the panacea some people think. The process is labor-intensive and expensive and necessarily involves decision-making: what to preserve and what to discard?

Research involves assembling an array of facts, some useful, some not so much, and then cobbling them together in a way that the author hopes makes sense, a way that provides new insight into a story that readers think they already know. Starting a project, it is impossible to know what information will be incorporated into a future book or magazine article. Maintaining a complete history of the sport depends on preserving everything, not just selected articles, letters or photographs. The "discard" pile sometimes includes the most valuable information.

Source material for this book included *Blood-Horse* and *Thoroughbred Record*, the leading weekly trade journals covering Thoroughbred racing at the time. *Blood-Horse* continues publication today in print and digital versions; *Thoroughbred Record* later morphed into *Thoroughbred Times* and then went out of business entirely in 2012. The Keeneland Library acquired the magazine's extensive clipping and photography files when the assets of *Thoroughbred Times* were sold at public auction. Photography archives from both publications provided many of the illustrations for this book.

Daily Racing Form did—and still does—provide the most thorough day-to-day reporting on Thoroughbred racing in the United States. The Keeneland Library houses one of the few, if not the only, complete *Daily Racing Form* and *Morning Telegraph* archives in existence. The library is in the process of digitizing the complete collection, a monumental task that eventually will provide online access to the papers. The project is worthy of support from anyone whose vocation or avocation involves horse racing.

Reporters from the *Courier-Journal* in Louisville and the *Herald-Leader* in Lexington provided extensive coverage of the Triple Crown.

The late Jim Bolus was a prolific journalist and author who wrote extensively about Thoroughbred racing in general and the Kentucky Derby in particular. His collected papers are archived at the Derby Museum in Louisville, Kentucky, and were a treasure-trove of information.

Motion picture producer and director Salomon Gill recorded extensive interviews with Pedro Baptista Jr., whose father owned Cañonero II; Juan Arias, who trained Cañonero II; Gustavo Ávila, who rode the horse; and many other individuals who played roles in the story. He shared those interviews, some in English, some in Spanish. José (Omar) Aracena, director of administration and operations for the Racetrack Chaplaincy of America, and Israel Avelar, assisted with translations.

The Ballad of Cañonero II is an award-winning documentary film focusing on the horse's losing bid for the Triple Crown in the 1971 Belmont Stakes. It was one of the first films to utilize multiple cameras to photograph a horse race and includes original music and interviews with Juan Arias and Gustavo Ávila.

YouTube has become the ubiquitous source for video recordings of just about everything imaginable, and the 1971 Triple Crown races are no exception. The quality of the videos isn't always the best, and the race calls sometimes are in Spanish, but actually seeing the surprise of Cañonero II's come-from-behind win in the Derby, the record-setting victory in the Preakness, and the horse's game but losing effort in the Belmont are worthwhile supplements to even the best written descriptions of the Triple Crown races. Suggestions are:

1971 Kentucky Derby: http://www.youtube.com/watch?v=mLv8Rvno_L4
1971 Preakness Stakes: http://www.youtube.com/watch?v=pqBP1KSvx_o
1971 Belmont Stakes: http://www.youtube.com/watch?v=DtHdWTMejqg

An excellent video about the 1966 Epsom Derby, won by Charlottown with Cañonero II's sire, Pretendre, finishing second, can be viewed at http://www.britishpathe.com/video/the-derby-4.

Separating fact from fiction in the fairy tale story of Cañonero II isn't always easy. Much of what was written about the horse during his 1971 Triple Crown campaign, especially in the days before and after the Kentucky Derby, was a rehash of previous stories. Contradictions and inaccuracies kept cropping up in various articles, eventually taking on a life of their own. Finally, they were accepted as fact.

Aside from a few perfunctory mentions prior to the race, the press generally ignored Cañonero II before his upset win in the Derby, so the typically thorough prerace reporting accorded the favorites was absent. No one in the Cañonero II camp at Churchill Downs for the Derby spoke English, which further complicated matters for reporters facing tight postrace deadlines. Reliable interpreters were at a premium, and almost by default, the first articles that made it into print after the race—questionable translations and all—became "reliable" sources for future coverage.

There was some very good contemporaneous reporting about Cañonero II throughout the Triple Crown, of course. Edward L. Bowen, managing editor at *Blood-Horse* magazine, and Whitney Tower, who covered horse racing for *Sports Illustrated*, come immediately to mind. Columnists Joe Hirsch and Herb Goldstein, along with their colleagues at the *Daily Racing Form*, quickly made up for lost ground as interest in Cañonero II's quest for the Triple Crown grew. It would be impossible to tell Cañonero II's story without the work of these turf writers.

Steve Haskin is senior columnist at the *Blood-Horse*. More than anyone else, Steve has kept Cañonero II's memory alive for the last forty years, and he was the first person I contacted when work on this book got underway. I wanted to be certain that Steve did not have his own book on Cañonero II in the works—he didn't—and to ask whether he could point me in the right direction for more information—he could. Thanks, Steve, for your help and for agreeing to write the foreword. And most of all, thanks for introducing me to Salomon Gill.

Sal is a motion picture producer and director whose California-based Celestial Filmworks has a feature-length film about Cañonero II and the colt's quest for the Triple Crown in the works. The movie has a working title of *Viva Cañonero!* and is scheduled for release in late 2014. Watch for it!

Sal generously offered to share his research material for the film, including lengthy interviews with Pedro Baptista Jr., Juan Arias and Gustavo Ávila, the owner, trainer and jockey, respectively, of Cañonero II. Sal's wealth of material resolved many of the perplexing inconsistencies in contemporary press reports and added important details to Cañonero II's story. When contemporary reporting did not jibe with personal recollections, I tended to go with the latter.

Omar Aracena, director of administration and operations for the Racetrack Chaplaincy of America, assisted with translations of the taped interviews when my Spanish was not up to the task, which was almost always. The Racetrack Chaplaincy provides vital support to the farm and backstretch workers who are essential to horse racing, and the organization deserves the thanks and support of everyone in the Thoroughbred industry. Israel Avelar helped me make sense of a number of Spanish-language websites and gave me a better understanding of the importance of Cañonero II to Thoroughbred racing in Venezuela.

In the years since its inception, the Keeneland Library has become the most important resource for anyone conducting serious research into Thoroughbred racing's rich history. Director Becky Ryder, Librarian Cathy Schenck and everyone else on the staff truly hold the keys to the kingdom, and their assistance and support always are much appreciated. It's difficult to imagine writing anything about Thoroughbred racing without spending a lot of time at the Keeneland Library.

Chris Goodlett is curator of collections at the Kentucky Derby Museum at Churchill Downs in Louisville, Kentucky. The museum houses the papers of the late Jim Bolus, who may have written more about the history of the Kentucky Derby than anyone else. Chris sorted through the Bolus material for information on Cañonero II and came up with several bits of information that I couldn't have found anywhere else.

Anne M. Eberhardt, visuals director at *Blood-Horse*, is a longtime friend and excellent photographer who provided access to the magazine's extensive photo archives. Digital Assets Coordinator Kevin Thompson helped with image selection and also scanned a batch of photographs, making my life far easier than he realizes.

Edward L. Bowen was managing editor at *Blood-Horse* during Cañonero II's Triple Crown run. He also is the person who hired me to join the magazine's editorial staff in 1973, just before Secretariat's Kentucky Derby. Ed took time from his work as president of the Grayson-Jockey Club Research Foundation to recount his memories of Cañonero II's races.

Thanks to J. Banks Smither, commissioning editor at The History Press, who thought Cañonero II's story was one worth telling; to project editor Julia

Turner; and to everyone else who had a hand in editing and production. They're a wonderful group of professionals.

When my previous book for The History Press, *Noor: A Champion Thoroughbred's Unlikely Journey from California to Kentucky*, was released, an astute reader named Valerie Teti contacted me to point out a few factual errors. I came away annoyed (not at her, certainly, but at myself for letting errors slip through the editing cracks) and impressed with her knowledge and attention to detail. Thanks, Val, for casting a critical eye on the manuscript for this book.

Finally, my deepest appreciation goes to my wife, Roberta. I remain convinced that my writing always is more difficult for her than it is for me.

INTRODUCTION

W ere he alive today, Sigmund Freud likely would discuss dreams in clinical terms. He would describe the images as messages drifting up from a client's subconscious, messages representing the fulfillment of a wish, either obvious or repressed. The interpretation of dreams is a powerful tool in psychoanalysis, Freud could say with authority, having pioneered the field more than one hundred years ago. Dream interpretation, he wrote, "is the royal road to the knowledge of the unconscious in mental life."[1]

Were he alive today, Pedro Baptista Sr. almost certainly would disagree.

A deeply spiritual man, Don Pedro would say that dreams can be more than simple fodder for a therapist's musings. Dreams have power, he would argue, and sometimes the meaning of a dream is so clear that it needs no further interpretation from anyone beyond the dreamer.

One night early in 1971, Don Pedro experienced such a dream, vivid images in which his deceased mother told him that he would win the Kentucky Derby later that year with a horse named Cañonero.[2] That was the name Don Pedro had given to a three-year-old colt he had purchased as a yearling and that he had raced with modest success. Freud might have speculated that the dream was nothing more than the manifestation of a wish that every Thoroughbred owner harbored, hoisting the coveted gold Derby trophy in the winner's circle at Churchill Downs.

Even if accurate, though, that simplistic interpretation was irrelevant to Don Pedro's understanding of the dream. He never had dreamed of his late mother before, and the message she brought to him that night in Caracas was abundantly clear and strong. Unlikely as it might be, Don Pedro took the prediction to heart. This was not wishful thinking on his part. Don Pedro knew it would come to be, knew that his horse named Cañonero II would win the Kentucky Derby.

The problem was not interpreting the dream. The meaning was obvious. The problem, Don Pedro knew all too well, was the horse.

Cañonero II had won a couple low-level sprints in Venezuela as a two-year-old, but a late season foray to California (that was when the "II" had been appended to his name) had been a disaster. The colt ran a creditable race against allowance company in his Del Mar debut, finishing third, but he was outclassed when he faced the best juveniles on the West Coast in the rich Del Mar Futurity. Breezed twice on the morning of the Futurity[3] and perhaps getting a questionable ride in the afternoon, Cañonero ran fifth that day. Don Pedro first mentioned the Kentucky Derby to trainer Juan Arias during the flight from Venezuela to California. If Cañonero II won the Del Mat Futurity, or if he at least ran a decent race, Don Pedro said, the colt might be pointed toward the Derby.[4] That trip now looked unlikely.

Cañonero II was beaten by nearly eight lengths in the Futurity by June Darling, a filly that was at the top of his game in the late summer and fall of 1970. The Futurity winner was one of the best juvenile fillies of the year, ranked only one pound below champion Forward Gal on the Experimental Free Handicap. Fillies, even good ones, seldom run in the Kentucky Derby, however, and when they do, they almost never win. (Exceptions are Regret in 1915, Genuine Risk in 1980 and Winning Colors in 1988.) Running fifth in a race won by a filly, even a good one, is not the sort of outcome that usually fosters an owner's Derby dreams.

Don Pedro sent Cañonero II to the States hoping to find a buyer for the colt, and the scheme almost worked. Despite Cañonero's dismal showing in the Futurity, the colt attracted the attention of trainer Charlie Whittingham, who was in the process of developing another horse from South America, Cougar II, into a champion on grass. Negotiations stalled due to communication problems—no one who accompanied Cañonero II to California spoke sufficient English to seal the deal—and Whittingham finally gave up.[5] With no other potential buyers in sight, Cañonero II was returned to Venezuela.

A crooked-legged colt with an odd way of going, Cañonero II so far had shown nothing to suggest that he had Derby credentials worthy of a start in the most famous horse race in the world. To complicate matters further, unexpected setbacks had left Baptista's business in Venezuela teetering on the edge of bankruptcy. Financial problems were serious enough that Cañonero II raced in the name of Baptista's son-in-law, Edgar Caibett, as a ploy to avoid potential creditors' liens on the horse. It was ownership in name only, however, and it was common knowledge that Don Pedro made all the decisions for the stable.

A trip to Kentucky with Cañonero II was an expensive and risky gamble that would stretch the family's finances to the limit. Hardly anyone thought it was a good idea.

He was crazy to even think about running Cañonero II in the Kentucky Derby, Don Pedro's friends and acquaintances in Caracas cautioned him over and over, but their warnings fell on deaf ears. He ignored his well-meaning friends and the critical reporters and pressed on, springing the unexpected news on Juan Arias while setting his sights on Churchill Downs and the first Saturday in May. Don Pedro risked everything on a dream, on a young trainer who wasn't even sure that he could find Kentucky on a map and on one of the most improbable Derby horses ever to run, let alone finish first.

Amazingly, Cañonero II won. Don Pedro's dream was fulfilled.

Instantly famous in Venezuela, where the horse was hailed as a national hero after winning the Kentucky Derby and Preakness Stakes, Cañonero II quickly faded from the collective memory of most racing fans in the United States. It's an unfortunate, but understandable, oversight. After all, a horse that almost won the Triple Crown was easy to forget in a stellar decade that produced Triple Crown winners Secretariat, Seattle Slew and Affirmed.

For five glorious weeks in 1971, though, the dream of a man became the dream of a nation, and Cañonero II commanded everyone's attention as the most exciting racehorse in the world.

Part 1

THE CARACAS CANNONBALL

Chapter 1
DERBY OF THE MISSING

Never show up for a visit unannounced," newspaper advice columnists have urged the socially challenged over the years. "Call ahead first."

There actually is an etiquette rule against just "dropping in," Miss Manners says: "It dates from the invention of the telephone, which can be used to inquire whether a visit would be convenient, and the disappearance of the household butler, who could stoutly claim that madam was not at home."[6]

When a small van chugged up to the stable gate at Churchill Downs around noon on Saturday, just seven days before the 1971 Kentucky Derby, track superintendent Thurman Pangburn faced just such an unannounced—and completely unexpected—guest. Pangburn could count all the ribs on the rangy, bay colt standing inside, and he must have thought the pronouncement that Cañonero II had arrived to run in the Kentucky Derby was a mistake, or maybe just a bad joke.

Last-minute shippers from other tracks for the Derby were not uncommon. Impetuosity and Twist the Axe, first and second in the Blue Grass Stakes at Keeneland, had settled into their stalls a few hours earlier that day; Bold Reason was due in from New York on Sunday; and a flight carrying Unconscious from the West Coast was scheduled for Monday. But Cañonero II presented a problem that track officials were not prepared to address. No one expected the horse to run, hardly anyone had even heard of him and no advance stabling arrangements had been made.

Complicating matters further was a serious language barrier. The groom with Cañonero II, Juan Quintero, could speak no English, Pangburn had no command of Spanish and the influx of Hispanic workers that would forever alter the character of the backstretch was years away. After a few frustrating minutes, Pangburn went in search of an interpreter to help sort things out. If this bedraggled horse really was a Derby contender, no matter how unlikely that prospect seemed at the moment, Pangburn needed to find him a stall.

Cañonero II and Quintero waited, with as much patience as man and horse could muster after a twenty-four-hour, nonstop van ride from Miami to Kentucky. Happy just to be standing still, they were becoming accustomed to unexpected problems, and a few minutes stuck outside the stable gate was just another inconvenience, and a minor one at that, in a bizarre string of mishaps and near disasters.

It was an administrative and logistical miracle, enhanced by a healthy dose of good luck, that Cañonero II made it to Churchill Downs at all.

Horses do not simply show up a few days before the Kentucky Derby, their owners expecting a spot in the starting gate on the first Saturday in May, without some advance paperwork establishing eligibility to run. While Cañonero II's appearance at the stable gate was a surprise, he had been properly nominated for the race, and he would not be turned away. (Derby fields now are filled by horses that are nominated and that qualify to run under an evolving point system designed to weed out the obvious misfits. The "Road to the Kentucky Derby" for 2014 includes thirty-four races with qualifying points awarded to horses that finish first through fourth.[7] A similar qualification system operating in 1971 would have eliminated Cañonero II from the Derby field.)

Fulfillment of Pedro Baptista Sr.'s dream of a Derby victory with Cañonero II depended on getting the horse nominated for the race. With the deadline for the nomination hours away, one of Baptista's friends managed to locate Charles J. Lang Jr. in Miami. Lang was there drumming up nominations to the Preakness Stakes, a race that over the years had become merely a stopover between the Kentucky Derby and the Belmont Stakes. A third-generation horseman whose father rode 1929 Kentucky Derby winner Reigh Count, Chick Lang tirelessly promoted the Preakness and almost single-handedly converted the Preakness into a wildly successful weeklong festival with an identity all its own.

Waiting to have lunch with his wife, Nancy, and prominent Fasig-Tipton auctioneer John Finney, Lang got a phone call.[8]

"My phone rings," Lang told journalist Joseph J. Challmas, who was working on a book about the Preakness, "and the gentleman on the other end of the line said he would like to nominate a horse for the Kentucky Derby, the Preakness and the Belmont.

"I said, 'You would?'"

"He said, 'Yes, I would.'"

"What is the horse's name?

"He said, 'Cañonero the second. He's by…,' a series of strange names, odd names.

"And I said, 'Well, you know I'll take the nominations for you, but I have to have a little more information. Would you spell the horse's name?

"Well, he wasn't quite sure how to spell it. And he wasn't quite sure how to spell his sire's name. And I'm saying to myself, that S.O.B. You know if you got a horse, you know how to spell his name. It's like entering your daughter in a beauty contest and saying, 'I don't know how to spell her name.'"

Lang initially dismissed the phoned-in nomination as a joke. "Flimsy" is how he described the conversation with the man who had what sounded to Lang like a "phony accent." Neither he nor Finney had heard of a horse named Cañonero II, the sire, the owner or the trainer. Lang crumpled the piece of paper with the information he had jotted down during the call, but there was just enough doubt in his mind that he hesitated before tossing it in the trash. What if it was legitimate after all? He decided not to take the chance.

Lang filled out the nomination form for the Preakness and passed the information along to officials collecting nominations for the Derby and the Belmont. Then he forgot about Cañonero II and the bizarre telephone call for a little over ten weeks, until late on the afternoon of the first Saturday in May.

———————

What should have been a relatively simple direct flight from Venezuela to the United States for Cañonero II seemed doomed from the start. The first plane developed engine trouble early on, and the pilot was forced to return to Caracas. Cañonero II was unloaded from one aircraft and transferred to another, but in-flight mechanical problems struck again over the Caribbean. The flight was diverted to Panama, where there was a delay arranging a third plane. Cañonero II eventually wound up on a cargo flight bound for the United States with livestock and crates of raucous chickens and ducks—along with Juan Quintero—as his traveling companions.

As bad as the journey had been so far, things got much worse in Miami. Cañonero II arrived on American soil without the proper—and necessary—health papers. This would have been a problem under any circumstances, but the timing was especially problematic. A major outbreak of Venezuelan equine encephalitis (VEE)[9] was developing in Texas, and other strains of equine encephalitis had been diagnosed in a dozen states east of the Mississippi River and in Iowa. VEE never had been diagnosed in the United States before, and federal animal health authorities were stepping up surveillance efforts for the disease.

Cañonero II was dehydrated and probably a little airsick when he arrived in Miami, but he had no obvious signs of being a sick horse. Many infected animals show no overt symptoms of VEE, however, and Cañonero II was arriving without health papers from a South American country where a serious disease was endemic. The horse was a potential carrier ("amplifier" is the scientific term) until he received a clean bill of health from the United States Department of Agriculture. VEE already had a foothold in the United States, and the authorities were taking no chances.

After hours on the tarmac in stifling South Florida heat, Cañonero II finally was unloaded from the cargo plane and immediately moved to a nearby United States Department of Agriculture quarantine facility. Blood samples were drawn and sent to a laboratory in Beltsville, Maryland, for serological analysis, but clearing Cañonero II from quarantine would take a while. VEE is a mosquito-borne disease, and for four long days, the horse was confined to a small, screened-in stall with no opportunity for exercise.

When Cañonero II was released from quarantine, around noon on Friday, April 23, he was in terrible condition. His bay coat was dull and lifeless, he was down at least seventy pounds and he looked nothing like a serious Kentucky Derby contender.

Some accounts speculated that problems with the Miami-bound flights from Caracas, along with fear of their recurrence, prompted Baptista to decide instead on a van to transport Cañonero II to Kentucky. In reality, the decision was much more pragmatic than that. Money for the trip had run out, and there were no funds to pay for a flight to Louisville. A 1,200-mile van ride for Cañonero II wasn't a choice; it was a necessity.

Cañonero II's arrival at Churchill Downs a week before the Derby was noted (without any mention of the travel problems) in the *Daily Racing Form*. It was the first substantive mention of the horse in extensive prerace press coverage, and like many reports that would follow, there was a glaring error. No one had heard of Cañonero II's trainer, Juan Arias, and his name

Cañonero II made it to Churchill Downs after a nightmarish journey from Caracas to Kentucky. *Courtesy of* Blood-Horse.

was misspelled in print as "Juan Arios."[10] The gaffe was not repeated in subsequent reporting; that it happened at all was indicative of the general lack of information available to the press about Cañonero II and his Venezuelan connections.

Arias was dismayed at Cañonero II's physical condition when the horse's odyssey finally ended at Churchill Downs. In public, at least, the trainer was candid about his colt's chances. He told track officials that Cañonero II had lost "much weight and probably wouldn't run good, but we run him anyway since we are already here."[11] There was little choice in the matter, Arias could have added. Unless Cañonero II earned a piece of the purse, there was no money to ship the bedraggled colt back to Venezuela.

Thurman Pangburn finally tracked down someone who was willing to serve as interpreter and assist in sorting out the confusion surrounding Cañonero II's unexpected arrival. José Rodriquez, a native of Puerto Rico who was working on the backstretch as an assistant to trainer Jack Rosenthal, volunteered.

"I was glad to help them in any way I could," he said later, "because that's why we're here—to help each other, especially when you are in need."[12] The extent of Rodriquez's involvement in the 1971 Derby would expand over the years, in foggy memories at least. Twenty years later, a column in the *Louisville Courier-Journal* carried the headline "José Rodriquez' Bizarre Derby Win."

A stall was located—No. 11, Barn 41—and Juan Quintero got Cañonero II bedded down. The colt's barn was adjacent to Barn 42, the main Derby barn where horses shipping in for the race from other tracks usually were stabled. Through 1968, Derby hopefuls often were scattered around the backstretch, assigned to whichever stalls were available. Apparently lax stabling procedures and security came under fire after Dancer's Image was disqualified from first place and moved back to last for a failed medication test in that year's race, however. To beef up security on the backstretch, horses entered in subsequent Derbies were concentrated in a single barn as much as possible.

Several people shared the role of middleman during Derby Week, interpreting for Arias, reporters and track officials at various times, but it was Rodriquez who became the most visible front man for Team Cañonero. He was everywhere—hanging around the barn to answer questions, in the paddock prior to the Derby, helping a nervous Arias saddle the horse prior to the race, even leading Cañonero II into the winner's circle. Arias missed what typically is a trainer's moment in the sun, walking at the head of a Kentucky Derby winner, because he did not make it across the track in time. An often-told story is that a security guard didn't believe Arias was the trainer and denied him access to the winner's circle. Although Arias did have difficulties making his way through the crowd and a phalanx of security officers, it was Cañonero II's groom, Juan Quintero, who was knocked to the ground by a National Guardsman as Quintero ran to his horse in the winner's circle.

To most observers, Rodriquez probably appeared to be Cañonero II's trainer, with Arias serving as the assistant.

Or, more likely, people simply assumed that the black man accompanying Cañonero II was the horse's groom. Arias was, after all, one of very few black men on the Churchill Downs backstretch who held a position of responsibility above that of groom or hot walker. He might have been the only one, although records are sketchy and it's impossible to be certain about his status. It had been twenty years since a black man had saddled a horse for the Kentucky Derby, though, and President Benjamin Harrison had been in the White House the last time a black man sent out a Derby winner.[13]

Like many urban areas, Louisville was a profoundly race-conscious city in 1971. Only four years earlier, equal housing demonstrators had threatened the unthinkable, a disruption of the Derby to gain national attention for their cause. Clashes between civil rights supporters and the Ku Klux Klan seemed inevitable, and Churchill Downs came to resemble an armed camp after a strong contingent of the National Guard was called out to help state police maintain order.

The anticipated trouble did not materialize. Civil rights marches were canceled at the last minute, and longshot Proud Clarion won a race unmarred by demonstrations. Public resentment over a threat to Kentucky's signature sporting event lingered long after the fact, however. A black man at the racetrack in the early 1970s typically held down a menial job. This was true in reality and, more importantly, in the collective mind of a predominantly Caucasian racing establishment. The color of his skin made it acceptable for a man like Arias to rub a Derby horse, but it was unthinkable that a black man might actually train one.[14] Arias clearly had his work cut out for him, winning with Cañonero II while battling years of prejudice.

Nominations to the Triple Crown races closed on February 15, 1971, with the following numbers: the Kentucky Derby, 220 nominations (a record at the time); the Preakness Stakes, 179 nominations; the Belmont Stakes, 166 nominations.[15] Given the conventional wisdom that practically conceded the first Triple Crown since Citation to Mrs. Stephen C. Clark Jr.'s unbeaten Hoist the Flag, it's a wonder that any other owner even bothered with sending in nominations to the three races.

Exceptional horses often create small fields. Only five other three-year-old colts could be mustered to challenge Citation in the 1948 Kentucky Derby, for example, and conversations about Hoist the Flag put the colt in the same exalted class as the Calumet Farm star. A strikingly handsome son of Tom Rolfe out of Wavy Navy, a winning mare sired by Triple Crown winner War Admiral, Hoist the Flag outraced his blue-ribbon pedigree. His juvenile

Hoist the Flag, juvenile champion in 1970 and the presumptive favorite for the 1971 Kentucky Derby, before his career-ending injury. *Courtesy of Keeneland/*Thoroughbred Times.

season lasted only a month, from a maiden win in early September through a first-place finish in the rich Champagne Stakes on October 10, and he never strayed from Belmont Park. Hoist the Flag finished the year unbeaten in four starts, although he was disqualified in the Champagne for causing a serious traffic jam during the early going. Hoist the Flag was placed last in the Champagne, a disqualification that cost the colt's owner $145,025.

Losing the Champagne on a technicality tarnished Hoist the Flag's stature not a whit. He was voted champion juvenile male at the end of the year, and Thomas Trotter, handicapper for the Jockey Club, considered Hoist the Flag to be the best of the year's juveniles. Of the 168 two-year-olds weighted on the 1970 Experimental Free Handicap, Trotter assigned Hoist the Flag the top weight of 126 pounds.[16]

Hoist the Flag started his much-anticipated run to the 1971 Kentucky Derby and beyond in March, with wins against allowance company (by thirteen lengths at Bowie, in the fastest time of the meeting for six furlongs) and in the Bay Shore Stakes (by seven lengths at Aqueduct). Hoist the Flag won the Bay Shore "easily" according to the chart caller for *Daily Racing Form*, his final time just four-fifths of a second slower than Dr. Fager's track record for seven furlongs. After the Bay Shore, Hoist the Flag's regular jockey, Jean Cruguet, was ecstatic, and unintentionally prophetic, about Hoist the Flag: "I don't think he'll ever get beat unless he falls down."[17]

An offer to syndicate Hoist the Flag for $4 million was rejected. His coronation was anticipated and expected, and his value would only increase.

Years later, Cruguet would call Hoist the Flag "the best horse I ever rode, by far. It wasn't Seattle Slew. [This was something of a surprise because Cruguet won the Triple Crown with Slew in 1977.] The first time I ever got on Hoist the Flag, I told everyone I knew that I was going to win the Kentucky Derby with this horse. The only reason I didn't say 'Triple Crown' was because I was so new in this country I didn't even know what the Triple Crown was. I'd never heard of it."[18]

Winter book bettors agreed with Cruguet's assessment. One of the few places to make an early wager on the Kentucky Derby in 1971, legally anyway, was through the future book operated by Agua Caliente Race Track in Tijuana, Mexico. Hoist the Flag had been a prohibitive winter book favorite for months, and in late March, after the Bay Shore, Caliente bookmakers lowered the odds on Hoist the Flag from three to one to even money. Among the other top three-year-olds, Executioner was four to one, Jim French and Unconscious were six to one, Eastern Fleet and Run the Gantlet were ten to one, five horses were fifteen to one and thirteen horses were twenty to one.[19]

A winter book bet on an unknown horse like Cañonero II, in the unlikely event that there was one so far in advance of the Derby, would pay off at odds around five hundred to one. Future book odds on Cañonero II would drop to three hundred to one and later to one hundred to one, still far above the on-track return for a winning bet on the horse.[20] If there had been a Cañonero II bandwagon, no one was jumping aboard.

The character of the 1971 Derby chase changed dramatically a few minutes after 9:00 a.m. on the morning of March 31, when trainer Sidney Watters Jr. gave Cruguet a leg up onto the back of Hoist the Flag for a workout in preparation for the colt's next start, in the Gotham Stakes. Watters told Cruguet to breeze Hoist the Flag for three-eighths of a mile and then keep him galloping for another five furlongs.

Hoist the Flag was the best horse Watters had ever trained, and the former steeplechase rider lost sleep trying to anticipate and forestall any problems. The March 31 workout was scheduled relatively late in the morning, when most horses already had been out, to give Hoist the Flag an opportunity to gallop over a track just harrowed and watered by the Belmont Park maintenance crew. It was all part of a meticulous schedule laid out for Hoist the Flag, and there was no reason to think anything could go wrong—until something did.

Just beyond the five-eighths pole, Hoist the Flag stumbled. Horsemen often say that a horse "took a bad step," but that description is far too benign for what happened to Hoist the Flag. Cruguet muscled the colt to a stop after the horse took several lurching strides and hopped off, but the damage had been done. Hoist the Flag shattered the long pastern bone and fractured the cannon bone in his right hind leg. The coffin and sesamoid bones also had been fractured.

Watters told famed sports columnist Red Smith:

> I can't believe it really happened. I deliberately waited until the harrows came on the training track. We broke him off at the mile pole where there was virtually no traffic, and worked him around the three-eighths pole. He did just what we wanted him to do—five-eighths of a mile in 1:02. He had done his work and was pulling up at the quarter pole when I saw Jean trying to pull him up. I sensed that something was wrong because we had intended to gallop him out to the finish line.
>
> It was a perfect strip. A horse hadn't been on it. I guess he just put his foot down wrong.[21]

Dr. Mark Gerard, the first veterinarian to examine Hoist the Flag after the accident, said that the injuries were the worst he had ever seen. The colt's ankle, Dr. Gerard said, "felt like a bag of loose rocks the size of marbles." He ordered a set of radiographs but told Watters that it was an "obvious destruction case." A veterinarian representing Lloyd's of London, the giant insurance conglomerate that had written a mortality policy on the colt for $500,000 dollars, agreed with the preliminary assessment and gave permission to have Hoist the Flag euthanized.

Informed of the accident and the gloomy prognosis in a telephone call from Watters, Mrs. Clark said to "save the horse at any cost, as long as he doesn't suffer."[22]

Quickly assembled was a team of surgeons that included veterinarians Drs. Jacques Jenny, William O. Reed, Donald Delehanty and Gerard, along with human orthopedic surgeon Dr. John Keefer. They toiled over Hoist the Flag's injured leg until late in the night at Dr. Reed's equine hospital at Belmont Park. Screws were inserted where there was enough undamaged bone for the threads to grip; a metal plate secured with more screws and wire further stabilized the pastern area. A radiograph of the ankle looked more suited to Dr. Frankenstein's monster than to a horse that, a few hours earlier, had been the prohibitive favorite for the Kentucky Derby.

The first fiberglass cast immobilized Hoist the Flag's leg from hip to ankle, leaving the colt standing on his toe, a straight line running from the horse's hip to the ground. A second cast, more bulky than the first, returned the ankle to a more normal angle.

Six weeks later, Dr. Gerard said that Hoist the Flag probably would lose mobility in the injured ankle, but that he was "cautiously optimistic" about the prospect of the colt being sound enough for stud duty.[23]

Quantity in the Derby was no longer a question after the loss of Hoist the Flag; with the favorite out, the field would be a large one, packed with

Get-well cards addressed to Hoist the Flag arrived at Belmont Park after the surgery to save the horse's life. *Courtesy of Keeneland/*Thoroughbred Times.

horses whose owners had renewed hope. Quality, on the other hand, was a real issue. Hoist the Flag's injury garnered the most attention because of his stature, but as the field for the ninety-seventh Derby sorted itself out, it became clear that few of the top two-year-olds of 1970 would be facing the starter at Churchill Downs.

Of the juveniles weighted on the 1970 Experimental Free Handicap, none of the top twelve would run in the Derby.[24] This was not uncommon—only one of the last five previous Kentucky Derby winners had been weighted on the Experimental as a two-year-old—but the consensus nevertheless was that with no standout, the 1971 Kentucky Derby was a race that any horse could win.[25]

Had Hoist the Flag stayed sound, he almost certainly would have started as the odds-on favorite in a relatively small field. With Hoist the Flag suddenly and unexpectedly on the sidelines, though, three-year-olds started coming out of the woodwork in the weeks before the race. As Derby Day approached, the projected field grew to twenty horses, maybe twenty-one, maybe more. Whatever the final number of starters, it would be one of the largest fields in the history of the race, possibly the largest. It was a turnout that some people thought was too large for the track to safely accommodate.

Prior to the 1971 Kentucky Derby, only seven runnings in ninety-six years had attracted fields of twenty horses or more: 1923 (twenty-one horses, won by Zev), 1925 (twenty, won by Flying Ebony), 1928 (twenty-one, won by Reigh Count), 1929 (twenty-one, won by Clyde Van Dusen), 1937 (twenty, won by Triple Crown winner War Admiral) and 1951 (twenty, won by Count Turf). Cañonero II's Derby would be the eighth.

Large fields would become more common in the post–Cañonero II years. Since 1971, there have been ten fields with twenty or more horses: 1974 (twenty-three horses, the Centennial running won by Cannonade), 1981 (twenty-one, won by Pleasant Colony), 1983 (twenty, won by Sunny's Halo), 1984 (twenty, won by Swale), 2005 (twenty, won by Giacomo), 2006 (twenty, won by Barbaro), 2007 (twenty, won by Street Sense), 2008 (twenty, won by Big Brown), 2010 (twenty, won by Super Saver) and 2012 (twenty, won by I'll Have Another).

A large field doesn't always indicate a weak field, but the pre-Derby perception was that 1971 was going to be one of those years when it did.

Columnist Mike Barry wrote that there were "plenty of bad horses" in the field. He picked Cañonero II to finish eighteenth. "This one's from Venezuela," Barry wrote, "which is a long way to come to finish a long way back."[26]

Barry's fellow columnist, Dean Eagle, called the 1971 running "the Derby of the missing."[27]

Central Kentucky turf writer Frank T. Phelps wrote that "this was probably the poorest Derby field since Tim Tam won in 1958."[28]

Overlooked in the shuffle, Cañonero II was given little chance. One Derby Day tip sheet, representing the weight of popular opinion, dismissed the colt completely: "Unknown factor from Venezuela who just got out of quarantine. No horse from abroad has ever won the Derby and he doesn't figure to make history. 100-1."[29]

What the touts and hardly anyone else knew, due in part to the slow arrival of complete past performance information from Venezuela, was this:

Of the twenty horses that would face starter Jim Thomson in the ninety-seventh Kentucky Derby, only one already had carried the scale weight for males in the Derby (126 pounds) and won; only one horse had run at the Derby distance (one and one-quarter miles) and won; and only one horse had run and won against older horses.

That horse was the unheralded Cañonero II.

TWO INDIANS AND A BLACK

Plucked from the familiar confines of the Hipodromo La Rinconada on the outskirts of Caracas, where he had achieved a measure of success as an up-and-coming young trainer, Juan Arias roamed the Churchill Downs backstretch a stranger in a strange land.[30] His perpetual smile masked a growing frustration. Arias was isolated by a language barrier, and he felt ignored and ridiculed by the press and just about everyone else.

His training methods, unorthodox by American standards, became the punch line for jokes, and he was portrayed as something of a likeable, and laughable, backstretch buffoon. When invitations went out for the annual Derby Trainers' Dinner, Arias didn't receive one. When entries were drawn for the Derby, Cañonero II was placed in the six-horse mutual field, lumped together with other three-year-olds accorded little chance in the race by the track handicapper.

Calumet Farm trainer Reggie Cornell commented to a reporter that he never had seen so much "garbage" in the Derby.[31] The insult infuriated Arias when word of the comment got back to him.[32] The trainer could deal with criticism aimed in his direction, even if it did leave a sizeable chip on his shoulder that lingered long after the race. But he loved Cañonero II, and knocks against his horse were far more painful.

The final indignity, although Arias had no way of knowing it at the time, involved post-Derby travel plans for his horse. The flight for horses shipping from Louisville to Baltimore for the Preakness was overbooked. One horse would have to be bumped, and a pre-Derby decision already had been

Cañonero II at Churchill Downs. *Winants Brothers photo. Courtesy of* Blood-Horse.

made—the horse to be bumped would be Cañonero II.[33] Like the comedian Rodney Dangerfield, neither Arias nor Cañonero II could get any respect.

Adding to the trainer's mounting concern was the physical condition of his Derby horse.

When Cañonero II stepped off the van from Miami, with the Derby just a week away, the colt was in sad shape. Gaunt and dehydrated after a hellacious journey from Venezuela, the curve of Cañonero's ribs showed through a coat that was dull and lifeless. The horse looked less like a legitimate Kentucky Derby contender and more like the embarrassment most people predicted he would be. Juan Arias faced a daunting task, getting Cañonero II ready for the sternest test of the horse's life while trying to nurse the colt back to health.

Complicating matters further, travel funds were running perilously short. Arias reached into his own pocket more than once to advance a few dollars in meal money to Cañonero II's groom and even found himself in the embarrassing position of haggling over the cost of feed for the colt. Informed by a feed dealer that the asking price for a sack of bran was five dollars, Arias shook his head from side to side and asked if he could buy only a half-sack.

He finally relented and handed over five dollars after he was assured that he could take any leftover feed with him after the Derby.[34]

Scrimping and cutting corners were nothing new for Arias, a man whose life had been a constant struggle to escape crippling poverty. Like Pedro Baptista Sr., Arias was chasing an unlikely dream with Cañonero II.

Born in Marin, a tiny village situated in a rich agricultural plain at the foot of the Andes Mountains in western Venezuela, Arias grew up in a Caracas slum. His father abandoned the family when Juan was young, and he was raised by his mother, sister and grandmother. He still kept a room at the home of his extended family while he was training Cañonero II.

Arias became enamored of horses and racing as a youth. Instead of leaving home to see a movie or to play with friends as he usually told his mother, he often would steal away to the Hipódromo Nacional El Paraíso and muck stalls for free. Arias wound up at Churchill Downs with a Derby horse years later because of his perseverance in the face of one obstacle after another and because of an unlikely confluence between his interests and those of military strongman General Marcos Pérez Jiménez. Although Arias never met the brutal dictator, which probably was fortunate for the trainer, both men had one important thing in common—they loved Thoroughbreds and horse racing.

General Jiménez took power in oil-rich Venezuela through a military coup in the late 1940s. Over the next decade, he fashioned a repressive regime that became known for rigged elections, corruption on a massive scale and lavish excess. He was embraced by the U.S. government for his willingness to sell Venezuela's oil at bargain prices and ridiculed elsewhere as the poster child for a Third World despot. While slashing funds for education, healthcare and other essential public works, General Jiménez spent exorbitant sums on bizarre projects. He built a replica of Rockefeller Center and what was supposed to be the world's most expensive military officers' club in a luxurious mountaintop hotel overlooking Caracas.

The general also built a racetrack, one of the best in South America.

The Hipódromo La Rinconada on the outskirts of Caracas carried a price tag of $80 million, a staggering figure in the 1950s.[35] By comparison, it cost only $32 million to completely renovate Belmont Park in New York a decade later. Both La Rinconada and the Belmont Park renovation were designed by famed racetrack architect Arthur Froehlich, whose work also can be seen at tracks in Canada, Panama, Trinidad, France and South Africa. On a wall in his California office, Froehlich hung a photograph that showed the architect touring the site where La Rinconada would be built with General Jiménez.

"Take a close look at that photograph," Froehlich told a reporter. "The president and I are the only ones not carrying machine guns."[36]

A sprawling complex with three grandstands, barns, dirt and turf courses, elegant bars and restaurants and a state-of-the-art veterinary hospital, La Rinconada opened on July 5, 1959. Ironically, General Jiménez never saw a race at the track he built. He was deposed in a coup eighteen months earlier, and he fled the country, along with an estimated $250 million he had skimmed from Venezuela's treasury. Crowds danced in the streets of Caracas when word of the general's ouster from power spread. Later in 1958, anti-American demonstrators stoned the motorcade of Vice President Richard M. Nixon in protest of U.S. support for the dictator.

Of more immediate benefit to Juan Arias than a new racetrack was General Jiménez's decision to start a government-sponsored school for aspiring local trainers. The dictator was distressed that foreigners were winning many of Venezuela's major races, Arias told *Sports Illustrated*'s Billy Reed.[37]

"The idea was to produce some Venezuelan professionals. At the time, the top trainers in the country were from England, Mexico, Peru and other countries," said Arias. Arias attended the school from 1955 through 1959 and received his trainer's license on July 4, 1959, the day before racing began at La Rinconada.

Arias trained what few horses he could hustle for the next few years, but he had little success.

"The only horses that I had I got by force," Arias told Reed, "and they were dogs. It was terrible. I slept in the barns and I didn't know where my next meal was coming from. Most of my classmates quit training pretty soon, and they advised me to quit, too. I guess the only reason I kept going was because I was young and single." For Arias, fretting over the cost of a bag of feed was a way of life.

Arias's career finally turned a corner in 1967, when a mutual friend introduced the young trainer to Pedro Baptista Sr. A well-to-do Caracas industrialist and an enthusiastic Thoroughbred owner, Baptista had a large number of horses that, like Arias, weren't winning very many races. Baptista decided to take a chance on Arias despite his dismal record as a trainer, and he gave the young man a few horses for a three-month trial.

Arias started winning with Baptista's horses almost immediately, bringing in some 700,000 bolivars in purses during the probationary period. The owner apparently was satisfied; by the end of 1967, Arias had the entire Baptista stable in his barn. The next year, Arias sent out the first three finishers in a major race for fillies at La Rinconada. It was Baptista's "greatest thrill in racing," the owner told Billy Reed.

Juan Arias was even more excited than the owner about the one-two-three finish in the filly race, Baptista added. Arias was "so loco that I had to get a doctor for him."

"A scuffler" was how Edward L. Bowen, managing editor of *Blood-Horse* magazine at the time, described Arias.[38] Bowen did not intend to disparage the trainer with the comment, just the opposite. He appreciated the fact that nothing ever had come easily for Arias, that every victory the man had won had been a struggle. It was an apt description of Arias and of Cañonero II.

As the ninety-seventh Kentucky Derby inched closer, attention finally shifted away from the horses that were not in the race—notably 1970 juvenile champion Hoist the Flag (injured), stakes winners Good Behaving (not nominated) and His Majesty (injured) and Flamingo Stakes winner Executioner (sound and eligible, but held out of the Derby in favor of future races by owner Peter Kissel)—and settled on those three-year-olds actually ready to run on the first Saturday in May. Conventional wisdom about the supposedly weak field notwithstanding, there were some very nice horses on the grounds at Churchill Downs.

Arthur A. Seeligson Jr.'s Unconscious was the best the West Coast had to offer. The horse had a record of four first-place finishes and one second from five starts as a three-year-old in California, winning a pair of stakes races at Santa Anita and taking the California Derby at Golden Gate Fields in near-record time his last time out. The colt would go to the post as the betting favorite at odds of nearly three to one.

Frank J. Caldwell's well-traveled Jim French was one of the favorites for the Derby, primarily off a fast-closing win over Unconscious in the Santa Anita Derby on April 3. Mostly, though, Jim French was consistently almost very good. The colt managed a handful of near misses in stakes races while shuttling around the country—from Tropical Park, to Hialeah, to Aqueduct, to Gulfstream Park, to Santa Anita, back to Aqueduct and then on to Churchill Downs. With Hoist the Flag out, Jim French almost by default became the Caliente winter book favorite for the Derby.[39] It would start in the race as the five-to-one third choice. Jim French was the highest-weighted horse on the 1970 Experimental Free Handicap, with 118 pounds, to actually make it to Churchill Downs.

Jim French's pedigree was as interesting as his race record. He was sired by Graustark, a brilliant son of Ribot, which a few years earlier had drawn as much praise coming up to the Derby as Hoist the Flag. Graustark suffered a fractured coffin bone during a driving second-place finish to Abe's Hope in the Blue Grass Stakes. Like Hoist the Flag, Graustark survived his injuries to become a prominent sire.

Most intriguing of all the Derby horses, as much for their owner's back story as for their racing prowess, were the Calumet Farm entries of homebreds Eastern Fleet and Bold and Able. Calumet already had seven Derby trophies in the farm office outside Lexington, Kentucky, and an eighth was up for grabs in court.

Calumet homebred Forward Pass finished second in the 1968 Derby, soundly beaten by Dancer's Image. The winner's postrace urine test apparently turned up positive for phenylbutazone, an analgesic now widely used but subject to a zero tolerance policy at the time under Kentucky's Rules of Racing. Attorneys for Peter Fuller, owner of Dancer's Image, challenged the validity of the drug test and five years of legal wrangling ensued to determine the official winner of the race.[40]

Mrs. Lucille Markey, owner of Calumet Farm, thought Forward Pass deserved the Derby trophy, the farm's eighth. Disgusted with the delay, she said that Calumet would never race in Kentucky again because of the disputed finish. She kept her word for two years.

"I can't see the point in racing where I can't win," she told writer Jim Bolus. "When a horse is disqualified, he's disqualified. We've been disqualified before and we've always accepted it."[41]

The Calumet owner later softened her self-imposed boycott: "I never said I wouldn't ever race again in Kentucky. I just said I wouldn't race there until a decision was made one way or the other."[42] She rescinded the boycott entirely when Eastern Fleet and Bold and Able came along and looked like serious Derby contenders, although a final decision awarding the 1968 Derby trophy to Forward Pass still was two years away. The power of a good horse or two in the barn can never be underestimated.

Eastern Fleet was considered the better of the two Calumet horses on the strength of a narrow victory over Executioner and Jim French in the rich Florida Derby and a second-place finish in the Wood Memorial. Good Behaving won the Wood, but he wasn't nominated to the Derby. Then Bold and Able rallied in the stretch to win the Stepping Stone Purse by three lengths a week before the Derby, with Eastern Fleet a lackluster sixth in a seven-horse field. Handicappers might have been baffled over Eastern Fleet's sudden reversal in form, but it is difficult to bet against a horse carrying Calumet's devil red silks in the Kentucky Derby. The Calumet entry was the second choice at four to one.

The only other Derby horses to start at odds less than ten to one were the entry of Impetuosity and Twist the Axe, first and second in the Blue Grass Stakes at Keeneland (six to one); List, winless as a three-year-old but second in Bold and Able's Stepping Stone (nine to one); and the much-maligned "mutual field" that included Cañonero II (also nine to one).

So-called straight betting typically involves a wager on only one horse to win, place or show. There are a few times, however, when a single wager involves more than one runner. When horses race for the same owner, such as Calumet Farm's Eastern Fleet and Bold and Able, they often are coupled in the betting as an entry, so a single two-dollar bet to win on the Calumet entry would pay off if either horse won the race. The same holds true for horses with different owners, but with the same trainer.

The mutual field, on the other hand, is not based on commonality of owner or trainer. Instead, the commonality among the field horses is a perceived lack of racing class. The field is made up of horses that the track handicapper thinks have little chance to win. Field horses were a necessity for the 1971 Derby for two reasons: the large number of horses in the race and limitations in the parimutuel equipment common to Churchill Downs and other racetracks. The Tote board showing odds for horses in a race could only accommodate twelve betting interests. The twenty-horse field in 1971 included eight individual horses (accounting for eight betting interests), six horses comprising three two-horse entries (another three betting interests) and six other horses in the mutual field (the twelfth, and final, betting interest).

The longest shots in a race usually are lumped together in the mutual field, and a two-dollar bet to win on the Derby field in 1971 would pay off if any one of six horses won the race. That seldom happens. Prior to 1971, the only field horses to win the Derby were Flying Ebony (in 1925) and Count Turf (in 1951).

The half dozen field horses were a motley crew: Cañonero II, Barbizon Streak, Knight Counter, Jr.'s Arrowhead, Fourulla and Saigon Warrior. They had a collective record of nine wins from forty starts as three-year-olds, and one, Fourulla, was still a maiden. Field horses and maidens win the Derby with about the same frequency, although one horse that broke its maiden in the race, Sir Barton in 1919, became the first Triple Crown winner.

Even if the field horses were longshots, getting six horses for a single wager was an attractive wagering option for many bettors looking for a

Despite the lack of fanfare that accompanied the horse's arrival at Churchill Downs, Cañonero II had a few supporters prior to the ninety-seventh running of the Kentucky Derby. *Courtesy of* Blood-Horse.

two-dollar flyer. Quantity generally wins out over quality, and the odds on the field almost always are shorter than the odds would be on any individual field horse.

Backers of Cañonero II at Churchill Downs, and there were a few, were shortchanged by the colt's inclusion in the mutual field. Mike Battaglia, the track handicapper who set the opening odds for the Derby, later speculated that Cañonero II would have started at odds of one hundred to one if he had raced uncoupled from the rest of the field horses.[43] With no option other than a wager on the six-horse field, successful bettors would receive $19.40 for a $2.00 ticket to win. In New York off-track betting shops, where the field horses were listed as individual betting interests along with the other Derby starters, a winning ticket on Cañonero II would pay three times as much.

If Cañonero II had raced uncoupled from the rest of the field, he likely would have challenged Donerail, winner of the 1913 Kentucky Derby at odds of ninety-one to one, as the longest shot ever to win the race.

The 1959 Royal Palm Handicap was supposed to be an easy gallop for four-year-old Nadir. Bred and raced by Arthur B. Hancock Jr.'s Claiborne Farm, Nadir won the richest race in the world as a two-year-old in 1957, the Garden State Stakes in New Jersey, and he shared juvenile championship honors that year with Jewel's Reward. The son of Nasrullah won the American Derby in 1958, and he was a logical choice as the odds-on favorite in the one-and-one-eighth-mile Royal Palm.

Hialeah bettors looking for an easy score were disappointed. Nadir got within a half length of the lead in the stretch in the Royal Palm but could get no closer. He faded to third, more than two lengths behind surprise winner Petare. Dismissed at odds of fifteen to one, Petare had shipped in from Venezuela to Miami a few days before the race. The eight-year-old had been in the United States only five days, and out of quarantine only three, when he won the Royal Palm. There was no stall for the horse at Hialeah, so he trained for the race at nearby Tropical Park.

Petare probably benefitted from the change in elevation, from more than three thousand feet in Caracas to sea level in south Florida. Athletes, both human and equine, typically experience a temporary boost in performance when they compete at sea level after training at higher altitudes. This is one of the reasons why the U.S. Olympic Committee operates a training center near Colorado Springs, Colorado. The improvement can be short-lived, however, as the athlete acclimatizes to the lower elevation.

Altitude aside, Petare's win in the Royal Palm was due in large part to a well-judged ride from Gustavo Ávila, a young jockey on the way to becoming one of Venezuela's premier riders. Nicknamed El Monstruo—"the Monster"—for his aggressive riding style and his uncommon success with longshots, Ávila overcame initial bouts of nerves to be the leading apprentice in Venezuela in 1956, his first full year riding. He was the country's leading jockey overall in 1957, 1958, 1959, 1967 and 1973. He retired from riding in 1985, with 1,472 victories to his credit.[44]

Ávila was a star in his own country, and he had far more name recognition in the United States than either Cañonero II or Juan Arias, who had none. In addition to his win with Petare in the Royal Palm, Ávila rode Venezuelan classic winner Prenupcial to a third-place finish in the 1961 Washington, D.C. International at Laurel Race Course in Maryland, competing against a field of very good horses and Hall of Fame jockeys. Prenupcial was outrun that afternoon by grass champion T.V. Lark (ridden by John Longden, in course-record time) and the great Kelso (with Eddie Arcaro in the saddle)—not bad company. In 1966, Ávila won the inaugural Clásico Internacional del

Caribe, the most important race for three-year-olds coming from a dozen Caribbean countries.[45]

Owned by a Caracas history professor named A.A. Dorato, eight-year-old Petare was a star in Venezuela but an unknown in the United States before Ávila brought the horse home a winner in the Royal Palm.[46] Pedro Baptista Sr. approached Ávila about riding Cañonero II in the Kentucky Derby, hoping El Monstruo could work his magic with another unknown horse from Venezuela. It was an easy choice for Don Pedro. Ávila had international success, and he already had won with Cañonero II at La Rinconada. Maybe most important, though, was the Indian heritage the two men shared and the trust Baptista had in the rider.

"Ávila," Don Pedro asked. "Do you want to win the Kentucky Derby?" It was a loaded question for any jockey. "Then get ready to fly."[47]

***

Although hardly anyone noticed amid the hoopla that accompanies every Kentucky Derby, the cool spring mornings in Kentucky (and a course of electrolytes to help overcome dehydration) were agreeing with Cañonero II. The shine was coming back to his coat, he was picking up much of the weight he had lost in quarantine and he was looking better and more fit every day. Relaxed and seemingly oblivious to the fact that the most important race of his life was just days away, Juan Arias refused to be rushed with Cañonero II. He adopted a more holistic approach instead.

Arias grazed the colt at every opportunity and sent him out for long walks and slow gallops, often with an uncommonly large exercise rider who rode with only a saddle pad, no racing saddle or no stirrups. He usually reserved full racing tack for serious workouts rather than for light exercise, feeling that his horses could tell the difference and anticipate an upcoming race. Trying to answer a reporter's questions, Arias would smile and pantomime a horse galloping. From time to time, he would press his face against Cañonero II's deep chest and speak to the horse softly in Spanish.[48] It was the way Arias always handled his horses in Venezuela, but it raised eyebrows among trainers who relied on a stopwatch and formulaic programs for their own Derby horses. It also made Arias an easy target for reporters who took potshots at the trainer and at Cañonero II. Years later, still stung by the criticism leveled at him by the press, Arias would deny that he ever "talked" to Cañonero II.

Juan Arias often sent Cañonero II to the track in the same way he trained the horse in Venezuela, with an exercise rider and no saddle. *Courtesy of* Blood-Horse.

In a week littered with fast training times, Cañonero II had only one published workout at Churchill Downs. In fact, according to *Daily Racing Form* past performances, the colt had only one published work anywhere, an omission that everyone knew could not be true. Cañonero II's most recent works in Venezuela, before the horse began his arduous trek to Kentucky, had been seven furlongs in 1:27 and one and one-eighth miles in 1:56. Neither time was especially fast—the La Rinconada racing strip was deep sand and tiring on a horse—and the workouts were too far removed in time to have much significance.[49]

Cañonero II's past performances were incomplete due to difficulties obtaining current racing information from Venezuela. All that was available for the colt's last three starts prior to the Derby were a few basic facts and a cryptic notation: "Further information not available." Bettors knew that Cañonero II had won four of eight races as a three-year-old but not very much else. The lack of reliable data was another reason, although most bettors did not need one, to dismiss the colt from Venezuela.

Three days before the Derby, over a sloppy track, Ávila breezed Cañonero II four furlongs in $0{:}53\frac{4}{5}$. The pedestrian effort did not impress anyone, with the possible exception of Arias, and he was not commenting about the workout in a language understood by most reporters. A clocker afterward told the trainer that "this is no Derby horse. You people are crazy."[50] Arias merely smiled.

It was a spectacularly slow time, especially when compared to other pre-Derby workouts.

List, not known as a speed horse, worked the same distance, over the same sloppy track as Cañonero II, more than three seconds faster. In fact, every horse that worked four furlongs any morning during Derby Week went faster than Cañonero II, sometimes much faster. Four-furlong times for other field horses Knight Counter ($0{:}46\frac{4}{5}$), Barbizon Streak ($0{:}47\frac{3}{5}$) and Saigon Warrior ($0{:}47\frac{3}{5}$) were the best; Eastern Fleet breezed four furlongs in $0{:}47\frac{3}{5}$; and Jim French clocked $0{:}48\frac{1}{5}$ at Belmont Park.

Beyond stating the inarguable fact that Eastern Fleet's four-furlong time was more than six seconds faster than Cañonero II's, meaningful comparison of training times is difficult. There are too many variables, especially when workout times on different days rather than race times when horses and riders presumably are trying their hardest are involved. A shopworn handicapper's axiom that one-fifth of a second is equal to one length suggests that Cañonero II was some thirty lengths slower than Eastern Fleet going into the Derby, based on their respective workout times. Not everyone agrees with the rule of thumb, however, and evaluating the two times in such a simplistic fashion is comparing apples to oranges.

There could be no argument about one thing, though. By any standard, Cañonero II's work was uncommonly slow for a horse's final Kentucky Derby prep.

Arias shrugged off the criticism of his horse's indifferent workout, with good reason. What no one knew about at the time, what was not revealed until much later, was Cañonero II's other workout, the secret one that occurred two days before the Derby.

With only one horse to train and hours of free time on his hands, Arias generally did not rush to the track at the crack of dawn like most of the other trainers. No one noticed when he made an exception on Thursday, two days before the Kentucky Derby. Early in the morning on April 29, under cover of darkness and with no one else around, Arias slipped a plain saddlecloth on Cañonero II's back and tightened the overgirth on Ávila's tiny racing saddle. He lifted the jockey onto the horse's back and sent them to the track.

It was an obscenely early hour, and the clockers' stand was empty—but it wouldn't have mattered. Without an identifying saddlecloth, Cañonero II was just another nondescript bay horse galloping through the dark.

Cañonero II worked three furlongs that morning in 0:35. Or possibly 0:34⅘.[51] The workout hadn't happened, officially, at least. It never showed up in Cañonero II's past performances and memories fade over time. Either way, it was the fastest time at the distance for any Derby horse in the week leading up to the race.

The clandestine workout answered any questions that Arias and Ávila might have had about whether Cañonero II truly belonged in the Kentucky Derby. The horse did. Any lingering doubts in their minds were erased by the rider's experience aboard another Derby contender.

Ávila knew Angel Penna, a trainer from Argentina who was preparing William A. Levin's Bold Reason. One morning, Penna asked his friend to exercise the colt. "Do you want to ride the next winner of the Kentucky Derby?" Penna asked Ávila. After galloping Bold Reason, Ávila confidently told Arias that Cañonero II was faster than Bold Reason and would win the Derby if Penna's horse was the best of the competition.

The biggest crowd in the history of the Kentucky Derby—123,284— packed Churchill Downs on May 1 for the ninety-seventh renewal of the storied race. At least the crowd was described as a record. It was difficult to be absolutely certain because 1971 was the first year in which track officials announced an "official" attendance figure. Prior to 1971, Derby Day attendance was given in vague terms, usually "around 100,000" people. How many actually showed up was anyone's guess.

On-track betting also set records, $6,389,567 for the day, $2,648,139 on the Derby alone. At the time, it was the most money ever wagered on a single horse race anywhere in the world.[52] Another $1 million was wagered on the Derby at off-track betting shops in New York, and untold millions changed hands through illegal bookmakers.

There is no way to really prepare a horse, or a first-time trainer, for the electric atmosphere in the saddling paddock at Churchill Downs on Derby Day. Cañonero II was tense and jumpy in the cramped area, and Arias was too nervous to saddle the horse himself. José Rodriquez took over that task at the last minute. In the excitement of the moment, no one noticed an imposing Texan standing off to the side, watching Cañonero II with a practiced eye. Robert Kleberg Jr. already had raced two Derby winners in his King Ranch colors, Triple Crown winner Assault and Middleground, and he knew a thing or two about a nice horse.

"That No. 15 is just about the best-looking colt I ever saw," Kleberg told *Sports Illustrated* writer Whitney Tower. "Who is he, anyway?"[53]

One of the most exciting moments in all of sports comes when the horses for the Kentucky Derby make their way from the paddock onto the track to the strains of Stephen Foster's *My Old Kentucky Home*. Conspicuously absent in the post parade in 1971 was Hoist the Flag, the presumptive Derby favorite until his injury a few weeks earlier. Hundreds of miles away in New York, Hoist the Flag was fighting for his life. By coincidence, the first Saturday in May happened to be the day when the cast on Hoist the Flag's shattered leg was to be changed. Things went well until the colt tried to stand after the anesthesia wore off.

"Paralysis of the quadriceps set of muscles had set in, and he couldn't stand," Dr. Mark Gerard told writer Bill Rudy. "Fortunately, we had tried to anticipate anything that could happen and we already had a hoist and a sling and other special preparations made available by the New York Racing Association. He was kept in a sling for eight hours." The paralysis eventually subsided, and by the next day, Hoist the Flag was able to move around in his stall. It was a far cry from a post-Derby coronation as the best racehorse of the crop that everyone expected before Hoist the Flag suffered his catastrophic injury, but it was a victory nonetheless.[54]

The twenty-horse Derby field required two starting gates placed side by side at the head of the stretch, where the track widened from 80 to 120 feet from rail to rail. The main gate had room for fourteen horses, and the auxiliary gate handled the six-horse overflow. Jim Thomson, a Scotsman who was starting his fifteenth Kentucky Derby, was expecting trouble from Cañonero II, and he ordered a blindfold (a set of blinkers with closed cups) to help calm the colt. This was nothing new for Cañonero II, Arias explained.

"It has been that way always," the trainer said. "He gets nervous in the gate and that is a big help, to put the mask on him. It is not much to do it. It just helps him."[55]

It was Saigon Warrior, not Cañonero II, that caused problems before the start.

Saigon Warrior started in the third post position, near the rail. Shortly after the colt was loaded into the gate, he began rearing and kicking. Jockey Robert Parrott, the first rider who failed to make the Derby weight of 126 pounds since that weight became the standard for three-year-old colts and geldings in 1919, was tossed over the back doors of the starting gate and landed heavily in the dirt.[56] Parrott hurt his knee, and there was some question about whether he could continue. But finally he remounted. The number of starters and the antics of Saigon Warrior taken into account, Thomson got the large field away with few mishaps.

Bold and Able, dismissed as the weaker half of the Calumet Farm entry until his surprise win in the Stepping Stone Purse a week before the Derby, sprinted to the front from the No. 1 post position. The first time past the stands, the leaders were bunched together, with Bold and Able setting a fast pace on the rail and the field horses Barbizon Streak, Jr.'s Arrowhead and Knight Counter close behind. Bold and Able's stablemate, Eastern Fleet; favored Unconscious; and third-choice Jim French were farther back, in a tight knot of horses three lengths off the pace.

Calumet Farm's Bold and Able set the pace during the early furlongs of the Derby, while Cañonero II lagged far behind and out of the frame. *Winants Brothers photo. Courtesy of* Blood-Horse.

Bold and Able and stablemate Eastern Fleet dueled for the lead as the horses moved into the stretch for the final quarter mile. Gustavo Avila had Cañonero II (No. 15) moving fastest of all on the outside. *Winants Brothers photo. Courtesy of* Blood-Horse.

Gustavo Ávila had Cañonero II galloping along at the start when most people expected him to be at the finish, in the back of the pack, some twenty lengths behind pacesetting Bold and Able. After a half mile, the colt had only two horses beaten; after six furlongs, he had moved up a bit but still was in fifteenth place. The track announcer didn't even mention Cañonero II's name for the first time until the horses were moving into the backstretch, some fifty-six seconds after the start, when the race was almost halfway over. The colt was so far back at that point that he was out of the frame as television cameras focused on the leaders.

Cañonero II did not get another announcer's call until the field turned into the stretch for the final quarter mile: "And Cañonero the second is moving!"

Ávila had been riding high in the saddle, biding his time, but now he had Cañonero II in a higher gear, charging up on the outside, six or eight horses wide. The colt was moving fastest of all the horses, making up ground on leaders Eastern Fleet and Bold and Able with every stride. With a furlong to run, the finish was no longer in doubt. Ávila angled Cañonero II toward the rail, and the colt quickly drew away to win by a widening three and three-quarter lengths. Jim French sneaked up into second place, followed by Bold

Cañonero II began to draw away near the finish of the ninety-seventh Kentucky Derby. Jim French, Eastern Fleet and Bold Reason (left to right) are bunched together on the rail. Unconscious (blaze) and Bold and Able are next. *Winants Brothers photo. Courtesy of* Blood-Horse.

Cañonero II won by three and three-quarter lengths, with Jim French second and Bold Reason third. *Courtesy of* Blood-Horse.

Reason and Eastern Fleet. Unconscious, the favorite at odds of nearly three to one, never was a threat and finished fifth.

Cañonero II surprised just about everyone with his winning performance in the Derby. The other field horses ran as expected and only managed to beat each other: Barbizon Streak, Knight Counter, Jr.'s Arrowhead, Fourulla and Saigon Warrior finished sixteenth through twentieth in the twenty-horse field.

The winning time over the fast track, 2:03⅕, did not threaten Northern Dancer's record of 2:00. Watching the race, it is difficult to know whether Cañonero II was drawing away through the stretch or whether the other horses were falling back. In the end, the distinction did not matter. Of the 22,910 Thoroughbred foals registered in 1968,[57] only one was a Kentucky Derby winner. That horse was the unknown colt from Venezuela dubbed the "Caracas Cannonball" by the press—Cañonero II.

José Rodriquez (right) who acted as an interpreter for the Venezuelans, led Cañonero II into the winner's circle after the Kentucky Derby. Trainer Juan Arias had problems getting across the track and missed that part of the ceremony. *Winants Brothers photo. Courtesy of* Blood-Horse.

Trainer Juan Arias, jockey Gustavo Ávila and Kentucky Derby winner Cañonero II in the winner's circle at Churchill Downs. *Courtesy of Keeneland/*Thoroughbred Times.

Juan Arias sprinted toward the winner's circle as an outrider brought Cañonero II back by the stands. Ávila waved, and the stunned crowd cheered. Arias ran into a problem getting across the track and missed the opportunity to lead Cañonero II into the winner's circle. Jose Rodrqiuez was deputized for that job. Arias was at the colt's head for the ubiquitous winner's circle photographs, though, and he was resplendent, sporting a blue-and-white tweed coat, a hot pink shirt with a blue striped tie, white pants and shoes and flashing an infectious grin in every direction.

Several jockeys complained about traffic problems and bumping during the race. Angel Cordero Jr., who rode Jim French, said that he "couldn't have had a rougher trip. I was bumped badly coming out of the gate, bumped badly at the half-mile pole, and bumped again in the backstretch. At one time we were sixth and we got knocked back to eleventh. Then my horse came on again and we still could have won it…I never saw Cañonero II coming until it was too late."

"We got tangled with a few other horses on the track," added Impetuosity's rider Eric Guerin. "I figured we were all going down, me, Kenny Knapp [Helio Rise], Jimmy Nichols [List], [Mike] Manganello [Knight Counter]…there were just too many horses on the track. I had my colt about five feet off the rail and he was running beautifully. I hadn't even asked him to do a thing when I was just banged out of the race. No horse could have overcome all that trouble."[58]

Ávila had no complaints about traffic problems for the simple reason that he kept Cañonero II well off the rail and out of potential trouble. The path meant that the colt ran farther than the Derby's official one and one-quarter miles and father than any other horse in the race, but staying out of trouble was worth it to Ávila.

"It is the dream of every jockey to win the Kentucky Derby," he said with the assistance of an interpreter. "I thought he could win, because he showed he was a good horse in Venezuela. I think those races at one and one-quarter miles he ran in Venezuela helped him a lot. He showed he could go the distance then. He was slow at the start, but for the last six furlongs he was real strong.

"We were in the clear all the way, on the outside of horses, and had no trouble."[59]

At the postrace party, someone asked jockey Laffit Pincay Jr., who finished fifth with Unconscious, if the disappointment of losing with the Derby favorite was tempered somehow because a fellow Latin American jockey won. It was an uncommonly silly question to ask one of the most successful and competitive riders in the history of the sport.

"Not particularly," Pincay said. "The only Latin jockey I wanted to see win was me."[60]

Pedro Baptista Sr. missed seeing his dream transformed into reality.

Business setbacks had left the owner on the verge of bankruptcy, and he stayed at home in Venezuela. Edgar Caibett, in whose name Cañonero II raced, did not make the trip either, but that was expected. Caibett was Cañonero II's owner as a matter of convenience, and it was common knowledge in Venezuela that Don Pedro called all the shots for the colt.

The Baptista family was represented at Churchill Downs instead by Don Pedro's eldest son, eighteen-year-old Pedro Jr., who sold his beloved Dodge Dart automobile in Caracas to finance the trip to Kentucky. The winner's

Pedro Baptista Jr. stood in for his father, Cañonero II's owner, during the trophy presentation, along with trainer Juan Arias and jockey Gustavo Ávila. *Winants Brothers photo. Courtesy of* Blood-Horse.

share of the purse, $145,500, was a Derby record and pushed aside the family's financial problems for a while.

Don Pedro had to learn about Cañonero II's stunning Derby win third-hand, from a local reporter who telephoned the owner after talking to a friend in Miami who had news of the race. Derby Day in the United States that year fell on May 1, which also happened to be Dia del Trabajador, Venezuela's Labor Day. Because it was a national holiday in that country, there was no television, radio or newspapers, and for a while, Don Pedro had no idea that he was the owner of a Kentucky Derby winner.

When the reporter blurted out the news that "Cañonero won," Don Pedro thought it was a joke, one in very bad taste, and he angrily slammed down the receiver. The reporter called back and finally convinced Don Pedro that he was telling the truth. Weeping uncontrollably, Don Pedro strode from room to room in the empty house shouting "Cañonero" over and over, although there was no one there to hear him. It was the first of many telephone calls that Don Pedro received that evening.

His first stop after getting the news was at the home of his father, a man of seventy-two years who had no interest in horses but an abiding interest in his son. He understood the importance of Cañonero II's victory to Don Pedro, however, and to Venezuela, and soon he was sobbing along with his

NINTH RACE CD 45409 May 1, 1971

1 1-4 MILES. (Northern Dancer, May 2, 1964, 2:00, 3, 126.) Ninety-seventh running KENTUCKY DERBY. Scale weights. $125,000 added. 3-year-olds. By subscription of $100 each in cash which covers nomination for both the Kentucky Derby and Derby Trial. All nomination fees to Derby winner; $1,000 to pass the entry box, $1,000 additional to start, $125,000 added, of which $25,000 to second, $12,500 to third, $5,000 to fourth, $100,000 guaranteed to the winner (to be divided equally in event of a dead heat). Owner of the winner to receive a gold trophy. Closed Monday, Feb. 15, 1971 with 220 nominations. Value of race, $188,000. Value to winner $145,500; second, $25,000; third, $12,500; fourth, $5,000. Mutuel Pool, $2,648,139.

Index	Horses	Eq't	A	Wt	PP	¼	½	¾	1	Str	Fin	Jockeys	Owners	Odds to $1
Ven '70^{3}	—Canonero II.		3	126	12	16^{1}	18^{5}	15^{3}	$4\frac{1}{2}$	1^{3}	$1^{3\frac{3}{4}}$	G Avila	E Caibett	f-8.70
45233Aqu^{4}	—Jim French	b	3	126	10	10^{h}	11^{2}	10^{2}	7^{2}	$5\frac{1}{2}$	2^{2}	A C'dero Jr	F J Caldwell	4.80
45233Aqu^{5}	—Bold Reason	b	3	126	14	18^{6}	$16\frac{1}{2}$	12^{2}	9^{2}	6^{2}	3^{nk}	J Cruguet	W A Levin	18.30
45107CD^{6}	—Eastern Fleet	b	3	126	17	6^{2}	3^{h}	$2^{1\frac{1}{2}}$	$2^{1\frac{1}{2}}$	2^{h}	4^{h}	E Maple	Calumet Farm	a-3.80
45216GG^{1}	—Unconscious		3	126	8	7^{2}	6^{2}	5^{1}	5^{h}	$4\frac{1}{2}$	$5^{1\frac{3}{4}}$	L Pincay Jr	A A Seeligson Jr	2.80
45126CD^{1}	—Vegas Vic	b	3	126	7	13^{3}	13^{3}	13^{1}	$13\frac{1}{2}$	7^{1}	6^{nk}	H Grant	Betty Sechrest-C Fritz	19.30
45202Kee^{7}	—Tribal Line	b	3	126	15	15^{2}	14^{h}	17^{6}	$8^{1\frac{1}{2}}$	8^{2}	7no	D E Whited	J E-T A Grissom	80.80
45107CD^{1}	—Bold and Able	b	3	126	1	1^{h}	1^{2}	$1^{1\frac{1}{2}}$	1^{h}	3^{h}	8^{3}	J Velasquez	Calumet Farm	a-3.80
45107CD^{2}	—List	b	3	126	18	17^{h}	$17\frac{1}{2}$	14^{2}	$14^{1\frac{1}{2}}$	9^{2}	9^{3}	J Nichols	Mrs J W Brown	8.60
45202Kee^{2}	—Twist the Axe		3	126	11	$9\frac{1}{2}$	10^{1}	7^{1}	$6^{1\frac{1}{2}}$	10^{2}	$10^{1\frac{1}{2}}$	G Patterson	Pastorale Stable	c-5.10
45107CD^{5}	—Going Straight		3	126	2	11^{2}	8^{h}	6^{h}	10^{3}	12^{2}	11^{h}	O Torres	Donamire Farm	45.60
45203Kee^{7}	—Royal Leverage		3	126	5	19^{8}	15^{2}	16^{1}	18^{5}	11^{h}	12^{2}	M Fromin	P Teinowitz	b-41.60
45202Kee^{1}	—Impetuosity		3	126	20	$8^{1\frac{1}{2}}$	9^{2}	8^{2}	15^{1}	13^{h}	$13^{1\frac{1}{2}}$	E Guerin	W P Rosso	c-5.10
45170Kee^{7}	—Helio Rise		3	126	16	$12\frac{1}{2}$	12^{1}	9^{h}	11^{1}	14^{1}	14^{3}	K Knapp	R W, V-R T Wilson Jr	58.20
45126CD^{3}	—On the Money		3	126	9	20	20	20	$17\frac{1}{2}$	$15^{1\frac{1}{2}}$	15^{1}	M Solomone	Teinowitz-Schmidt	b-41.60
45107CD^{4}	—Barbizon Streak		3	126	6	2^{h}	5^{1}	11^{1}	12^{1}	16^{6}	16^{18}	D Brumfield	Mrs H J Udouj	f-8.70
45202Kee^{4}	—Knight Counter	b	3	126	13	4^{2}	$4^{1\frac{1}{2}}$	3^{1}	3^{1}	17^{6}	17^{11}	M Mang'llo	R Huffman	f-8.70
45126CD^{2}	—Jr's. Arrowhead	b	3	126	4	3^{h}	2^{1}	4^{1}	$16^{1\frac{1}{2}}$	18^{2}	18^{6}	A Rini	Walnut Hill Farm	f-8.70
45259GP^{3}	—Fourulla		3	126	19	5^{h}	$7\frac{1}{2}$	18^{3}	19^{4}	19^{4}	19^{14}	D MacBeth	A H Sullivan	f-8.70
45203Kee^{3}	—Saigon Warrior		3	127	3	14^{3}	19^{9}	19^{5}	20	20	20	R Parrott	C M Day	f-8.70

f-Mutuel field.

a-Coupled, Eastern Fleet and Bold and Able; c-Twist the Axe and Impetuosity; b-Royal Leverage and On the Money.

Time, :23, :46$\frac{4}{5}$, 1:11$\frac{3}{5}$, 1:36$\frac{1}{5}$, 2:03$\frac{1}{5}$. Track fast.

$2 Mutuel Prices:			
12-CANONERO II. (f-Field)	19.40	8.00	4.20
7-JIM FRENCH		6.20	4.40
8-BOLD REASON			12.60

B. c, by Pretendre—Dixieland II. by Nantallah. Trainer, J. Arias. Bred by E. B. Benjamin (Ky.).

IN GATE—5:42. OFF AT 5:42½ EASTERN DAYLIGHT TIME. Start good. Won ridden out.

CANONERO II., void of speed and unhurried for three-quarters, was forced to come to the extreme outside to launch his bid upon leaving the backstretch, continued to circle his field entering the stretch to take command with a bold rush in the upper stretch and was under intermittent urging to prevail. JIM FRENCH, allowed to settle in stride, moved up along the inside when launching his bid on the second turn, was forced to come out between horses entering the stretch, commenced lugging in to brush with BARBIZON STREAK, continued gamely to move through close quarters in midstretch, but could not reach the winner. JIM FRENCH came back with a cut on the coronet band of his right rear. BOLD REASON, badly outrun for six furlongs, moved between horses until forced to steady when blocked in the upper stretch, dropped to the inside when clear and finished with good courage. EASTERN FLEET, away alertly to gain a forward position along the inside, moved through in slightly close quarters leaving the backstretch, moved to the fore between calls in the upper stretch, commenced drifting out in the closing drive and gave way willingly. UNCONSCIOUS, never far back while along the inner railing, continued to save ground while moving into serious contention on the final turn, came out for the drive and had little left when the real test came. BOLD AND ABLE was sent to the fore at once, bore out entering the first turn, came back to the inside when clear to make the pace to the top of the stretch, at which point he dropped back steadily. LIST failed to enter contention while closing some ground in the late stages. TWIST THE AXE, in hand early, moved up along the outside after three-quarters to loom boldly on the final turn, but could not sustain his bid. IMPETUOSITY, breaking smartly from his outside position, continued slightly wide to midway down the backstretch where he was dropped in to move up between horses, was forced to check sharply when JR.'S ARROWHEAD dropped over at the half-mile ground, losing his action, and failed to recover when clear. BARBIZON STREAK, away in good order, was caught in close quarters entering the first turn, continued slightly wide and commenced dropping back after five furlongs. KNIGHT COUNTER was bumped and forced out entering the first turn. JR.'S ARROWHEAD came away alertly to gain a striking position along the outside, commenced lugging in at the half-mile ground and dropped back steadily. FOURULLA bore out badly entering the first turn.

Overweight—Saigon Warrior, 1 pound.

Scratched—Sole Mio.

Official chart of the 1971 Kentucky Derby. *Copyright circa 2013 by Daily Racing Form, LLC and Equibase Company. Reprinted with permission of the copyright owner.*

son. The two men drove to the cemetery and prayed over the grave of the elder Baptista's wife, Don Pedro's mother. The younger man's dream had come full circle.

Cañonero II's surprise Derby win was a shock to the mostly white, mostly male old-boys' network that governed racing in the early 1970s. Don Pedro relished his role in upsetting the sport's proverbial apple cart.

"Look here," he told a reporter a few days after the Derby, "we have come up here—two Indians and a black—with a horse that nobody believed in and we're destroying three hundred years of American racing tradition dominated by the flower and the cream of your society."[61]

Leslie Combs II, whose Spendthrift Farm consignment topped the Keeneland summer sales for years, agreed that Cañonero II's victory in the Kentucky Derby was good for racing. It was an unexpected sentiment from someone who exemplified Thoroughbred racing's blue-blood "establishment."

"This shows that a few millionaires cannot tie up the game or the big races," Combs said.[62]

A few days shy of his thirty-third birthday, Juan Arias was living out a dream of his own. His share of the winner's purse, a little under $15,000, was a small fortune in Venezuela in the early 1970s, but Cañonero II's victory meant far more to him than money. Even in his wildest dreams, the young man who grew up in a Caracas slum never could have imagined that one day he would be standing in the winner's circle at Churchill Downs with his hands on the bridle of a Kentucky Derby winner. Not as a groom, he would remind people years later, but as the trainer.

Twenty years later, upon his retirement from a decades-long career as a reporter and race caller, Cawood Ledford reflected on his best Kentucky Derby memories:

> *In all the years we did the backstretch, I have always had [footage on] the winner, even Chateaugay and the other longshots. But I did not have Cañonero II. You had to have an interpreter to go by the barn. I didn't give him any chance. He had already gone one and one-quarter miles, but he had sold for nothing at Keeneland and I just thought it was some romantic notion of a rich South American wanting to run in the Kentucky Derby.*
> *You need a Cañonero II in the Derby from time to time.*[63]

Chapter 3
NO LIZ TAYLOR

C añonero II became a part of the public consciousness with his convincing, albeit improbable, win in the 1971 Kentucky Derby, but the colt's story really began five years earlier in another derby, on another continent.

The 1966 Epsom Derby in England attracted a field of twenty-five, but in the final furlongs it was a two-horse race. Pretendre, cofavorite with Right Noble, had his nose in front for a few strides, but he was outrun in a driving finish by fast-closing Charlottown. Five lengths farther back in third place was Edward B. Benjamin's Black Prince II. Charlottown won the derby four-fifths of a second faster than Sea-Bird the year before, but Benjamin was more impressed with Pretendre.

"My horse ran third in that race," Benjamin recalled of the 1966 Epsom Derby, "and Pretendre was second. But if my jockey had gone to the rail, he would have blocked off the winner and Pretendre would have won."[64]

Pretendre's form tailed off after the Epsom Derby and late in the year, after running sixth in the St. Leger, he was sold to American Nelson Bunker Hunt for $425,000. Hunt said that he liked Pretendre because of his pedigree and because he had been "a good 2-year-old *and* a good 3-year-old." He imported the horse to Kentucky to stand the 1967 season at Henry White's Plum Lane Farm near Lexington. Pretendre stood at Plum Lane for three years, and then Hunt sent the horse to New Zealand for the 1970 breeding season. To accommodate the required six-month quarantine before entry into New Zealand, Hunt stood Pretendre at Coolmore Stud in Ireland in the spring of 1970 and then in New Zealand in the fall for breeding on that country's Southern Hemisphere schedule.[65]

Hunt had an ambitious plan for Pretendre. He was going to breed his own mares to the stallion during the Northern Hemisphere breeding season—February to June—and then bring their offspring back to the United States and Europe for racing. New Zealand mares then would be bred to the stallion during the Southern Hemisphere breeding season. Shuttling a stallion between spring breeding in the Northern Hemisphere and fall breeding in the Southern Hemisphere has become more common in recent years. Pretendre was one of the first "shuttle sires."[66]

Pretendre's first-year stud fee at Plum Lane was set at $3,500. Benjamin remembered Pretendre from the Epsom Derby as a "strong horse," and he was one of the first breeders to send a mare to the stallion. That mare was Dixieland II, a Benjamin homebred that the next year foaled Cañonero II.

Benjamin often tried to duplicate the breeding patterns of good horses, and Dixieland II was a product of that philosophy. Champion Nashua was

Pretendre, sire of Cañonero II. *Courtesy of Keeneland/*Thoroughbred Times.

a son of Nasrullah and out of a mare sired by Johnstown. Benjamin had a Johnstown mare of his own, Ragtime Band, and for several years, he bred her to Nantallah, a stakes-placed son of Nasrullah that he also owned. Dixieland II was a product of one of those matings. It was not an exact match to Nashua's breeding, but it was as close as Benjamin could get. He said that he bred Dixieland II to Pretendre because the stallion was "a top stayer and an absolute outcross."

His optimism about the Pretendre–Dixieland II cross wavered in the fall of 1967, and Benjamin consigned the mare to the Keeneland breeding stock sale. Carrying a future Kentucky Derby winner, the mare was purchased by Claiborne Farm manager Bill Taylor for a modest $2,700—less, even, than Pretendre's stud fee. Benjamin boarded some of his mares at Claiborne, a historic breeding farm outside Paris, Kentucky, and Taylor bid on Dixieland II because he did not think Benjamin would want to see her sold so cheaply. After the sale, Taylor telephoned Benjamin and asked if he wanted Dixieland II back. Benjamin said that Taylor could keep the mare, but a couple months later he had a fortuitous change of heart.

"Bill," Benjamin said, "if you've still got that mare, I believe I would like to have her back."[67]

On April 24, 1968, at Claiborne Farm, Dixieland II foaled a bay colt with a star, a little white on a hind ankle and a crooked right front leg, a colt that would win the Kentucky Derby.

Benjamin had dispersed most of his Thoroughbreds in the mid-1950s, deciding to breed horses for the market in the United States and to race only in Europe. His six-horse consignment to the Keeneland sales in 1969—four yearlings in the summer select sale, two in the fall—included the most expensive yearling sold at auction that year and one of the cheapest. One of those yearlings would win the Kentucky Derby two years hence; the others would not.

Benjamin's sales topper at the 1969 Keeneland select sale was an attractive colt sired by 1958 Horse of the Year Round Table. Purchased by Mrs. Bert W. Martin for $210,000 and later named Knights Honor, the horse never amounted to much. He started four times without winning and returned almost nothing on his owner's hefty investment.

One of the most persistent, and demonstrably wrong, stories about Cañonero II is that he was rejected by the selection committee for the summer sale at Keeneland and wound up in the decidedly nonselect fall sale by default. Although Cañonero II probably would not have survived the selection process in any case, given his questionable conformation and mediocre pedigree, the colt was not rejected for the summer sale because he never was entered. There were no selection criteria for the fall sale where Cañonero II was catalogued; every horse that was entered was accepted.[68]

In a letter to turf writer and Kentucky Derby historian Jim Bolus some years later, Keeneland director of sales William S. Evans said this about Cañonero II:

> *CAÑONERO had an absolutely blank pedigree, both top and bottom, as a yearling. He was not entered for the 1969 July Sale. He was also not inspected by us prior to the September sale as we do not inspect the Fall yearlings. His poor pedigree, as well as his conformation, pointed to his $1,200 selling price. This was "catching lightning in a bottle."*[69]

The evening after the derby, Benjamin telephoned Carter Thornton, who owned Threave Main Stud near Paris, Kentucky. Benjamin boarded a few of his mares at Threave Main and Thornton had prepared Benjamin's auction yearlings in 1969.

"Do you remember what you recommended to me about that Pretendre colt?" Benjamin asked Thornton.

"Yessir," Thornton replied. "I told you he had a crooked right front, turned in from the knee down, and I recommended that you let him go in the fall sale. I saw him in the paddock today and he still looked crooked in front—but in the next two minutes or so it must have straightened out some, because he sure looked all right in the winner's circle."[70]

Evans was correct about there being little reason for buyers to look twice at the catalogue page for Hip No. 558 from the Benjamin consignment. Part of the problem was Cañonero II's pedigree itself, heavy with European bloodlines not in favor in America, but the abbreviated catalogue format also was a factor. Summarizing a horse's pedigree on a single page can be difficult, and shorthand conventions arose over the years to maximize the available information in the least space. Printing a horse's name in bold-face type to indicate a stakes winner is one of those conventions; emphasizing the dam's side of a horse's pedigree at the expense of the sire is another.

About Pretendre, the catalogue said only that the horse was a stakes winner, a half brother to another stakes winner and had been weighted second-high on the Free Handicap as a two-year-old. The races Pretendre won were not identified, and there was no mention of the horse's impressive near miss in the Epsom Derby. There was not sufficient information to attract the interest of a buyer who did not already know about Pretendre.

Buyers looking for black type on the distaff side of Cañonero II's pedigree had to drop down to the colt's fourth dam to find any stakes winners. A daughter of English stallion Hainault, unraced Baton was a decent producer. Her foals included three stakes winners and a horse that ran third in the Preakness Stakes, but the auction prospects of a horse with no selling points other than a nice fourth dam are slim. Potential buyers who got past the catalogue page and took the time to inspect Hip No. 558 probably lost interest as soon as they saw the colt.

W. Cothran Campbell, who pioneered the idea of syndicate ownership of Thoroughbreds, was one of those buyers. He talked recently about the sale with film producer Salomon Gill, who is working on a motion picture about Cañonero II.

"I was looking for likely candidates," Campbell said. He already was familiar with Pretendre's race record and knew Benjamin, so he stopped by the barn to take a look.

"This big bay horse came out of the stall," Campbell said, "and as he walked out, he was a knockout. I was crazy about him. But as he walked toward me I saw that he threw his right leg out. He had a crooked ankle. So I quickly told the boy to put him back in the stall." He made a terse notation in his sale catalogue, "right front," and crossed the colt off his list.

Campbell was in the front row of the Keeneland sales pavilion on Tuesday evening, midway through the four-day sale, when Hip No. 558 walked into the ring.

"He was still throwing that right foot out. Somebody paid $1,200 for him, and I thought, 'What a stupid thing to do' because the horse would never stand training. I congratulated myself for being so smart." Campbell years later framed the catalogue page with the hasty evaluation that caused him to reject a Kentucky Derby winner. "It keeps me down to earth," he said.

The "somebody" who bid $1,200 to get Hip No. 558 was Luis Navas, a bloodstock agent from Venezuela who made his living buying inexpensive horses in the United States and reselling them for a profit in South America. Signing sales tickets as "Albert, agent," Navas bought six yearlings at the 1969 fall yearling sale, spending a total of $11,800. The most he paid was $3,500, the least $900. There were cheaper horses sold that fall, a few in the $300 to $400 range, but Navas clearly was working the lower end of the sale

Property of Edward B. Benjamin

Barn

I

BAY COLT

Hip No.

558

Out of winning sister to Sawgrass (10 wins, $54,715), Cute Sweetie (8 wins, $40,975). Second dam winning half-sister to 5 winners. Third dam sister to BOATSWAIN, WAND (dam of HALBERD), KEARSARGE.

Foaled April 24, 1968

BAY COLT.....	*Pretendre.....	Doutelle........	Prince Chevalier
			Above Board
		Limicola........	Verso II
			Ucello
	Dixieland II....	Nantallah......	*Nasrullah
	(1961)		Shimmer
		Ragtime Band....	Johnstown
			Martial Air

By ***PRETENDRE**, stakes winner of 6 races in **England, second high weight on Free H. at 2.** Half-brother to stakes winner **Red Dragon.** His first foals are yearlings of 1969.

1st dam
DIXIELAND II, by Nantallah. Winner at 3 in England. This is her second foal. Her first foal is a 2-year-old of 1969.

2nd dam
RAGTIME BAND, by Johnstown. 3 wins at 4 and 5, $12,930. Dam of—
    Sawgrass. 10 wins, 2 to 9, $54,715.
    Cute Sweetie. 8 wins, 2 to 4, $40,975.
    Acceloro. 3 wins at 2, $13,710.
    Other winners: Hallatnan (2 wins, $9,375), Where's Mike.
    Mique's Miss. Dam of winners Little Sir (9 wins, $37,048), Red Royalty
        (8 wins to 5, 1969, $28,747), Miss Pilot (10 wins), Three E's.

3rd dam
MARTIAL AIR, by Man o' War. Sister to **BOATSWAIN, KEARSARGE, WAND.**
        Produced 5 other winners, including—
    Pibroch. 14 wins, 2 to 7, $31,830.
    Aero Jack. 4 wins at 4 and 6, $17,195.
    Trumpet Call. 4 wins at 4 and 5, $9,145. Dam of 5 winners.
    Magic Music. Unraced. Dam of 7 winners, including **Carrot Bunch** (15
        wins, 2nd Endurance H., etc.); granddam of **Musical Fury.**

4th dam
BATON, by Hainault. Unraced. Produced 5 winners, including—
    BOATSWAIN. 3 wins at 3, Withers S., 3rd Preakness S. Sire.
    WAND. 3 wins at 2, Matron S. Dam of **HALBERD, Caduceus,** etc.
    KEARSARGE. 4 wins at 3, Miles Standish S., 3rd Warren H. Sire.
    Baton Rouge. Placed at 2. Produced 5 winners, including **CREOLE MAID**
        (C.C.A. Oaks, dam of **NATCHEZ, Fais Do Do;** granddam of **TENDER
        SIZE**), **FIRETHORN** (sire), Rouge et Noir (dam of **CAILLOU ROUGE;**
        granddam of **JIMMY THE ONE, ACTIVE CRATER, NOTHIRDCHANCE**).

Engagements: Belmont Futurity 1970; Breeders' Futurity 1970; Pimlico-Laurel Futurity 1970; Del Mar Futurity 1970; Garden State Stakes 1970; Kentucky Jockey Club Stakes 1970; Arlington-Washington Futurity 1970.

Catalogue page from when Cañonero II was offered for sale at the 1969 Keeneland Fall Yearling Sale. *Courtesy of Keeneland.*

for his South American clients. Of the five yearlings sired by Pretendre in the fall sale, Cañonero II was the least expensive.

One-third of all the Thoroughbred yearlings sold at auction in 1969 went through the sales ring at Keeneland that fall. The sale grossed a record $5,168,500, the first time a fall yearling auction had topped the $5 million mark, with an average price of $4,448. Top price among the fall yearlings in 1969 was $95,000 for a filly sired by Hail to Reason. The top-priced colt was a son of Raise a Native that brought $60,000.[71]

The average price for Navas's six bargain-basement yearlings, $1,967, was substantially less than the overall sale average. Of his six purchases, three turned out to be winners: El Viajero (bought for $2,200), Cañonero II ($1,200) and the filly Comenve ($900). Cañonero II and Comenve were part of the package deal Navas put together for resale to Pedro Baptista Sr., and for a while, it looked as if the filly might be the better of the two. She consistently outran Cañonero II in morning workouts, but she could not duplicate those efforts in the afternoon and eventually was sold.[72]

Don Pedro paid $60,000 for the three-horse package from Navas, if reports in various publications can be believed. That figure almost certainly was wrong, by a large margin, possibly due to language problems or a misunderstanding about the exchange rate between American dollars and Venezuelan bolivars. A better estimate of Cañonero II's resale value as an unraced yearling was around $6,000.[73]

Cañonero II arrived in Venezuela in miserable condition, with a badly split hoof and a serious case of worms, and Juan Arias spent months nursing the colt back to health before he could start serious training. When Cañonero II finally made it to the races, in August 1970, the horse won a six-furlong, Series 9a handicap impressively by six and a half lengths. Racing in Venezuela had two programs, one for Venezuelan-breds and one for imported horses like Cañonero II. The idea was to prevent presumably better foreign horses from dominating all the races and winning all the purses at La Rinconada. Horses could move up from Series 9 to Series 8 by winning a race, and so on up through Series 4. The top three classifications, Series 3 through Series 1, were reserved for the best Thoroughbreds in Venezuela.[74]

After the ill-conceived trip to Del Mar, Cañonero II closed out the year with a win against Series 8a horses. The horse opened his three-year-old season winning a Series 7a sprint by five and a half lengths, and Don Pedro made the questionable decision to tackle better horses. Asking Cañonero II to move up from seven furlongs, the longest race he had run, to one and one-quarter miles in the Clásico Prensa Nacional was a predictable disaster. The colt finished eleventh in a field of twelve at the Kentucky Derby distance.

Cañonero II bounced back a week later to finish third in a Series 6a race at a mile and then won in three of his next five starts. In one of those races, at six and a half furlongs, the horse carried derby weight of 126 pounds and won; in another, he won at the Derby distance of one and one-quarter miles. Cañonero II's last race in Venezuela came on April 10, a few days before the horse was shipped to the United States. With wins at one and one-quarter miles and carrying 126 pounds, although admittedly not in the same race, Cañonero II already had accomplished things that no other horse he would face in the Kentucky Derby had done.

More important, the colt had shown that he responded well to the training of Juan Arias and that he got along very nicely with jockey Gustavo Ávila.

Edward B. Benjamin, breeder and seller of Cañonero II. *Courtesy of Keeneland/Thoroughbred Times.*

A reporter tracked down Edward B. Benjamin after Cañonero II's stunning win in the Kentucky Derby and asked the man who bred a Derby winner and then sold him for a pittance if he had any regrets about the sale. No regrets, no depression, Benjamin said. He was happy about Cañonero II's surprise victory and impressed with the colt he bred and sold.

"Bear in mind," Benjamin said, "that this horse was flown from Venezuela, and then vanned, mind you, *vanned*, from Miami to Louisville. He must have been twenty-five lengths better than the field to have won the way he did after that."[75]

The Derby was "just like *National Velvet*," Benjamin said, acknowledging the magic of the moment, "but without Liz Taylor."[76]

Chapter 4
ENCORE AT PIMLICO

J uan Arias still had a few things to prove and some critics to silence after the Kentucky Derby.

There was nothing new about that. Arias had been fending off doubters all his life.

Years earlier, when he was struggling to establish his reputation as a trainer in Venezuela, someone accosted him at La Rinconada with a stinging insult.

"You're not good for anything," the man said. "Where did you get your diploma from? Out of a box of talcum powder?" Arias stared at the man and then replied, "First of all, I don't depend on you for food. Second, it doesn't make any difference where I got my diploma. And third, someday I will prove that I am a better trainer than anybody."[77]

Arias was not there yet, not by a longshot, but with Cañonero II, he at least was attracting attention and was fast becoming a master showman on an international stage. But being a showman was far removed from the recognition he craved as a good trainer of Thoroughbreds. Winning the Kentucky Derby was a welcome addition to Arias's résumé, one that none of his contemporaries in Venezuela could claim, but it did little to convert the many nonbelievers in this country. Nor did it erase some hard feelings arising from the reception he and Cañonero II received in Louisville:

They made me feel like I was at the Derby to be a clown. They made fun of us at parties. There have been times when I wanted to tell the press to go to the devil, but I contained myself. Now I can do like your [John] *Campo*

Juan Arias and Cañonero II at Pimlico. *Winants Brothers photo. Courtesy of* Blood-Horse.

and go "bla, bla, bla!" Here in the United States the trainers think they know everything and that we trainers from other parts are supposed to be here to learn. I have shown these people a few things about training.

In the U.S., for instance, everyone trains by the stopwatch. Speed is the big thing. They train so much for speed that the horses get out there and crash into each other. But the stopwatch is a relative thing. In Venezuela I take every horse individually and train it according to its needs and to the requirements of the race.[78]

Arias tended to be secretive about the details of his training philosophy, and he made no mention of Cañonero II's unreported workout a couple days before the Kentucky Derby. That revelation would come much later. With scrutiny from the press heightened at Pimlico, Arias probably could not have staged a similar clandestine workout for the horse even if had wanted to do so.

Between Cañonero II's surprise win at Churchill Downs on the first Saturday in May and his race in the Preakness two weeks hence, the Derby raised as many questions for Arias as it answered.

Cañonero II under tack at Pimlico. *Winants Brothers photo. Courtesy of* Blood-Horse.

How could he convince the skeptics that Cañonero II's winning form in the Derby was something more than a fluke, more than a lucky accident brought on by a large field of horses that kept running into one another during the race?

How could he prove to the doubters, and there still were many, that his holistic training methods actually had merit?

How could he show that Cañonero II was the standout he believed him to be and that the colt belonged among the best Thoroughbreds of his generation?

And maybe most important, how could Arias silence his critics once and for all and prove that he belonged among the elite company of trainers he was keeping with Cañonero II?

The answer for Arias was very simple in concept and very complicated in execution. All he had to do was win the Preakness Stakes.

The experts who dismissed Cañonero II in the Kentucky Derby almost immediately began to search for reasons why the horse would not—could not—win the Preakness Stakes.

There would be a smaller field in the Preakness, they said, maybe half as many horses as Cañonero II faced in the Kentucky Derby. Eleven three-year-olds would pass the entry box at Pimlico, including the first four finishers in the Derby (Cañonero II, Jim French, Bold Reason and Eastern Fleet). Vegas Vic (sixth in the Derby) and Impetuosity (thirteenth) were the only other Derby starters to make it to Pimlico. With fewer horses, the traffic problems that supposedly benefitted Cañonero II in the Derby were less likely to occur in the Preakness, and the horse would have to win on his own merit. Many people still questioned Cañonero II's ability to do that.

The Preakness was shorter than the Derby by one-sixteenth of a mile, which they said would benefit speed horses like Eastern Fleet, Executioner and Sound Off at the expense of a come-from-behind runner like Cañonero II. The Derby winner had a stayer's pedigree and had won the Derby in a sweeping move on the final turn from almost twenty lengths back. The Preakness was too short for similar tactics to be successful.

The turns at Pimlico were too sharp for a big, long-striding horse like Cañonero II, they said. Whether or not there was any merit to that argument, Arias adopted it as his own at the annual Alibi Breakfast, held the morning before the Preakness. Originating in the late 1930s, when a group of trainers and owners would gather for coffee in the mornings and swap stories, some of them even true, about their horses, the Alibi Breakfast grew into an annual Preakness Week affair. Awards to members of the media and to other individuals prominent in racing were passed out each year, but the real function of the event was to allow trainers an opportunity to go on record with before-the-fact excuses in case their horses did not perform up to expectations the following afternoon.

"It will be difficult," Arias responded with the aid of an interpreter when asked about Pimlico's sharp turns. "The horse is so big [Cañonero II stood between 16.1 and 16.2 hands], it will be difficult for him."

"So he's off the hook," Jim French's trainer, John Campo, added, without the aid of an interpreter despite his New York accent.[79]

The Alibi Breakfast also hosted the presentation by Raymond Johnson, publicity director at Churchill Downs, of the $5,000 gold Kentucky Derby trophy to Pedro Baptista Sr. Johnson also handed out a smaller replica of the winner's trophy to Gustavo Ávila and an engraved gold stopwatch to Arias. The irony of the gift to Arias, a stopwatch bestowed upon a trainer who openly questioned the usefulness of such a timepiece for training horses, apparently went unnoticed.

There were other awards as well. Arias picked up a congratulatory Medallion of Merit authorized by the Congress of Venezuela and presented to the trainer in Washington, D.C., by the Venezuelan ambassador to the United States. Ávila received a similar medallion during a ceremony in Caracas, where he returned for a few days' rest between the Derby and the Preakness.

Cañonero II was, at best, a mediocre horse running against other horses from a mediocre crop, the "experts" said. Injured Hoist the Flag, Epsom Derby and Prix de l'Arc de Triomphe winner Mill Reef and a few others presumably were exempted from the label of mediocrity, but the scoffers were correct that Cañonero II wouldn't be facing those horses in the Preakness. Not that the strength of the 1968 foal mattered. Cañonero II did not have to be the best of the crop; the horse only had to be the best that showed up in Baltimore on May 15 for the Preakness Stakes.

That the current crop of three-year-olds was a weak one might have been the consensus, but the agreement about Cañonero II's place among the mediocre was far from unanimous. King Ranch owner Robert J. Kleberg Jr. had been impressed with Cañonero II when he saw the colt at Churchill Downs, and nothing had happened to change his mind.

"Cañonero just might be one fine race horse," Kleberg said before the Preakness.[80]

The supposed "acclimatization effect" that might have boosted Cañonero II's performance in the Derby would have worn off by the time the Preakness would be run, they said. There is a growing body of scientific evidence showing that the acclimatization effect is real, and that an athlete training at high altitudes experiences improved performance when competing at lower altitudes.[81] There is less agreement on how long the benefit lasts.

Hall of Fame trainer Horatio Luro told *Blood-Horse* magazine that he expected most horses coming to the United States from Venezuela would "run well right away, but then would lose their form. This would come about two to four weeks after arrival, and then many horses take from three to six months to become acclimatized."[82] Luro's math put Cañonero II in the danger zone for the Preakness and for the Belmont Stakes three weeks later. Cañonero II was not "most horses," though, and Arias seemed unconcerned.

Cañonero II was not getting enough serious work to be ready for the Preakness, they said. It was the same knock against the horse that critics made before the Kentucky Derby, and Cañonero II won that race going away.

Arias intended to work Cañonero II on Saturday, giving the colt five days to recover after a long van ride from Kentucky to Maryland. But the track was sloppy, so Arias delayed the work until the track was in better shape. A second delay ensued when Cañonero II went off his feed. A veterinarian was called in to extract two baby teeth. Cañonero II ran a slight fever and missed more exercise. The colt finally made it to the track for his first serious workout since the Derby on Wednesday, May 12. The Preakness Stakes was just three days away, and Arias was following the same seemingly lackadaisical training program he had employed prior to the Derby.

With Ávila in the saddle, Cañonero II worked five furlongs in a leisurely 1:06. Six other Preakness horses worked the same distance on Tuesday, Wednesday or Thursday, and all six had substantially faster times than Cañonero II. Vegas Vic's clocking for the distance was 1:00; Jim French worked in 1:00$\frac{1}{5}$ at Belmont Park; Bold Reason, also at Belmont Park, and Royal JD at Pimlico had times of 1:00$\frac{3}{5}$; Impetuosity covered five furlongs in 1:01$\frac{4}{5}$; and Preakness Prep winner Sound Off worked in 1:02$\frac{2}{5}$.

Arias called Cañonero II's workout a "speed test." *Daily Racing Form* called it "laughable."[83]

John Campo, Jim French's trainer, refused to criticize Cañonero II's slow workout.

"You don't change strategy because of time," Campo said at the Alibi Breakfast. "If he wins the Preakness, the Venezuelan is the best horse."[84]

On the flip side, support for Cañonero II's chances in the Preakness came from an odd source: Baltimore radiologist Dr. George Burke. After administering an electrocardiogram to Cañonero II at Pimlico, Dr. Burke pronounced the colt's heart rate "fantastic."

"He registered 30 heartbeats a minute on our portable EKG machine," Dr. Burke explained, "which is about a slow as a horse can go. I think his score of 30 compares favorably with the heartbeat of Jim Ryun, the famous miler. The normal beat in humans is in the 70 range. That's why his stamina is so great, but Ryun tested at 34."

Dr. Burke was not willing to make a prediction about the Preakness based on his research, but he did have an opinion about Cañonero II's physical condition:

"I'm a medical man, and I don't want to be placed in the position of being a handicapper. But I can tell you that Cañonero II is a dead fit horse insofar as his heart is concerned, and he should do well in the Preakness."[85]

Post positions were drawn on Thursday morning in the office of racing secretary Larry Abbundi. Jim French would start on the far outside, from post position No. 11. Cañonero II drew No. 9; Eastern Fleet and Executioner were side by side, in post positions No. 5 and No. 6, respectively.

Always the optimist, Campo did not think the outside post position would be a problem for Jim French.

"There is often less trouble on the outside," he said, "and the Preakness is a long enough race so that post position shouldn't make too much difference. The important thing is that he is doing well and he is honest. He'll give you his best race every time."

The track handicapper agreed with Campo's assessment of his horse and made Jim French the morning line choice at odds of five to two. Executioner, which ran a close second to Sound Off in the Preakness Prep after skipping the Derby, was second choice in the morning line at four to one. Cañonero II and Eastern Fleet were made the cothird choices at five to one.

Cañonero II won over some of the critics, but not all of them by any stretch of the imagination, with a stirring win in the Derby. The public, on the other hand, was beginning to embrace Cañonero II, and the colt's colorful entourage from Venezuela. By post time on Saturday, Cañonero II and Jim French were cofavorites at odds of slightly more than three to one. Executioner was the four-to-one second choice, and Eastern Fleet was third choice at six to one. Odds on the other seven horses ranged from Sound Off's eleven to one to Spouting Horn's eighty-one to one.

Jim French and the colt's brash native son trainer still held sway among New York bettors, who sent the horse off as the four-to-one favorite in the

Off-Track Betting pool. Cañonero II was the second choice in New York, at odds of five to one.

On Friday, the day before the Preakness Stakes, Cañonero II had a leisurely one-and-a-half-mile gallop over a muddy track, with Ávila in the saddle. It was the sort of training move that people had come to expect from Juan Arias, who said that Cañonero II's condition leading up to the Preakness was "perfectamente."[86] Later that day, Arias had Cañonero II walked from the Preakness Barn to the turf course, where horses for the race would be saddled the following afternoon. When Cañonero II's handler led the colt into the winner's circle, there was a round of applause. Optimistic as always, and planning ahead for the race itself, Arias said that he wanted Cañonero II to become accustomed to the "noise of the crowd and the sight of the cameras" after the victory.[87]

———•———

Any hope that the Preakness would be run more cleanly than the Derby vanished as soon as the starting gates sprang open. Eastern Fleet swerved sharply to the right and slammed hard into Executioner, which had been a faction slower breaking from the gate.

"He [Eastern Fleet] broke right into my mount," Jacinto Vasquez, who rode Executioner, said after the race. "I had to take my horse up."[88]

The two colts had collided in a similar fashion earlier in the year, at the start of the Florida Derby, but Executioner recovered on that occasion and ran a close second to Eastern Fleet. This time, though, Executioner did not fare so well. Thrown off stride at the start, the horse never was a factor and finished sixth. An inquiry into the bumping incident delayed the posting of the official order of finish for a time, but after reviewing film of the race, the Pimlico stewards let the original result stand.

Eastern Fleet was a speed horse that liked to run on the lead. After roughing up Executioner, jockey Eddie Maple let the colt go to the front as the field moved past the grandstand for the first time. He had a clear lead after the first quarter mile and still was a head in front after a half mile. Eastern Fleet's stablemate, Bold and Able, had set the early pace in the Kentucky Derby, but the horse was not entered for the Preakness. Eastern Fleet was on his own and things were going as most people expected. The early fractions were swift (0:23⅗ for the first quarter-mile and 0:47 for a half mile), the Calumet Farm colors were at the fore and Eastern Fleet seemed to be exactly where Maple wanted him to be.

Calumet Farm's Eastern Fleet was in front as expected the first time past the grandstand. The surprise was Cañonero II's bid for the lead on the outside, a length back. *Winants Brothers photo. Courtesy of* Blood-Horse.

Behind Eastern Fleet, though, a totally unexpected turn of events was developing.

Cañonero II had dawdled through the first six furlongs of the Kentucky Derby, so far out of touch with the leaders that the colt often disappeared from the frame in films of the race. Now Gustavo Ávila was hustling the big horse with the long stride and the stayer's pedigree toward the front, challenging the speedy Sound Off for second place behind Eastern Fleet. Cañonero II put Sound Off away going into the first turn, and after a half mile the horse was in second place, running head to head with Eastern Fleet.

The two colts matched each other stride for stride down the backstretch, Eastern Fleet running easily on the inside near the rail, Cañonero II on the outside with Gustavo Ávila almost standing in the irons taking a firm hold on the reins. Their strides were so evenly matched that from the stands the pair looked like one horse. After six furlongs in 1:10⅖, the rest of the field began to drop back. Eastern Fleet and Cañonero II had the Preakness Stakes to themselves.

Cañonero II pushed a head in front for good after a mile, battled a game Eastern Fleet through the stretch and finally drew clear in the final sixteenth to win by one and a half lengths. Jim French managed a lackluster rally

Left: Cañonero II still trailed Eastern Fleet on the first turn but was getting closer to the lead. *Winants Brothers photo. Courtesy of* Blood-Horse.

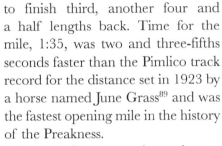

Bottom: Eastern Fleet and Cañonero II raced stride for stride down the backstretch. *Winants Brothers photo. Courtesy of* Blood-Horse.

to finish third, another four and a half lengths back. Time for the mile, 1:35, was two and three-fifths seconds faster than the Pimlico track record for the distance set in 1923 by a horse named June Grass[89] and was the fastest opening mile in the history of the Preakness.

Intermediate race times do not count as official records, but final times do. Cañonero II won the 1971 Preakness in 1:54, lowering Nashua's stakes record by three-fifths of a second. In the years between 1955 (when Nashua set the old Preakness record) and 1971 (when Cañonero II broke it), no other horse seriously threatened the mark. The three-year-olds that came the closest were Horse of the Year Damascus (1967) and Kentucky Derby winner Majestic Prince (1969), lofty company for Cañonero II.

Edward B. Benjamin was trying to approximate the bloodlines that had produced champion Nashua when for several seasons he bred his Johnstown mare Ragtime Band to

It was Eastern Fleet on the rail and Cañonero II on the outside at the head of the stretch. *Winants Brothers photo. Courtesy of* Blood-Horse.

Cañonero II began to pull away from Eastern Fleet at the eighth pole. *Winants Brothers photo. Courtesy of* Blood-Horse.

Near the finish, Cañonero II was a length in front. *Winants Brothers photo. Courtesy of* Blood-Horse.

Cañonero II defeated Eastern Fleet in track-record time. *Pimlico photo. Courtesy of* Blood-Horse.

Nantallah, a son of Nasrullah. Among the foals resulting from those breedings was Dixieland II, dam of Cañonero II. Although the Nantallah-Johnstown cross was a couple generations back in the pedigree of the Preakness Stakes winner and was not an exact match for Nashua's breeding, Cañonero II was living proof that the nick still was a good one.

There was dancing in the streets in Venezuela after Cañonero II crossed the finish line first in the Preakness Stakes. Without a holiday-imposed television and radio blackout, an estimated five million people—half the nation's population—watched the race on live television. Venezuelan president Rafael Caldera and members of his cabinet sent congratulatory telegrams to Juan Arias and Gustavo Ávila, and the Venezuelan ambassador to the United States hosted a raucous victory party for Don Pedro and his traveling party of a dozen friends, Arias and Ávila at the embassy in Washington, D.C.

Cañonero II's victory even managed to quell student rioting, a national pastime in its own right in many Latin American countries, for a few hours. The only hint of controversy, if you can call it a controversy, was a dispute over the propriety of a local television station's decision to use the Venezuelan national anthem for background music as Cañonero II crossed the finish line at Pimlico.[90]

"You can't imagine the impact this has had in Venezuela," Don Pedro said. "Cañonero II is truly a horse of the people, something the people can identify with."[91]

Everyone, apparently, loved Cañonero II.

"It has been a long time, indeed, since Venezuelans—all Venezuelans, the men in the streets, the people in the villages—have been so excited about anything as they are about the victories of Cañonero," a Caracas newspaper reported after the Preakness.[92]

Almost overnight, Cañonero II had become a national hero in Venezuela and a celebrity everywhere racing fans had access to television or a newspaper. The colt was an underdog-turned-hero in a sport that relishes improbable success stories, and Don Pedro, Arias and Ávila were being carried along on a magical ride of vindication and recognition.

The owner commented after the Preakness that he was disappointed because there was no official recognition of Cañonero II's record-setting victory. A few days after the race, before Cañonero II shipped out to New

Jockey Gustavo Ávila (second from left), Pedro Baptista Jr. (third from left) and Pedro Baptista Sr. (fifth from left) accepted the Woodlawn Vase, one of the oldest and most valuable trophies in all of sport history. *Winants Brothers photo. Courtesy of* Blood-Horse.

York for the Belmont Stakes, the colt finally was honored by Pimlico. Governor Marvin Mandel proclaimed that the owner, trainer and rider were honorary citizens of Maryland, and the Venezuelan national anthem was played as Cañonero II strutted onto the turf course. A standing ovation from some eight thousand fans in the stands affirmed that Cañonero II really was the people's horse.

Baptista, Arias and Ávila stood in the winner's circle, smiling, arms linked, soaking up the accolades. It was one of the last expressions of unity to come out of the Cañonero II camp.

Cañonero II's Preakness Stakes record would stand for thirteen years, until Gate Dancer lowered the stakes mark by two-fifths of a second, to 1:53⅗, in 1984.

Or maybe not.

Only five horses challenged Secretariat in the 1973 Preakness Stakes, understandable considering that the Meadow Stable colt had run the fastest Kentucky Derby in history two weeks earlier. Ecole Etage was the early leader in the Preakness, until jockey Ron Turcotte, who thought the pace was too slow, made a bold move with Secretariat on the first turn. Three horses wide and moving fastest of all, Secretariat charged from last place to first and drew clear. He won by two and a half lengths, with Sham second.

It was a spectacular effort by one of the greatest Thoroughbreds of all time. When *Daily Racing Form* selected the "Top 10 Preakness Stakes Moments" prior to the 2011 renewal of the race, "the Move" was at the top of the list. Cañonero II's Preakness was number ten on the list: "Those who figured that the Venezuelan colt Cañonero II was nothing but a fluke when he won the Derby were slapped with the bright reality of his record Preakness performance."[93]

Secretariat won the race in 1:55, at least according to the Visumatic timer's electronic readout on the Tote board in the Pimlico infield. This was a full second slower than Cañonero II's stakes record set two years earlier. The time seemed not to match the brilliance of Secretariat's race, however, and questions about the accuracy of the electronic timing device started circulating almost immediately. Two veteran clockers from *Daily Racing Form*, Frank Robinson and Frenchy Schwartz, working independently and from different vantage points, came up with identical—and significantly faster—times for the race, 1:53⅖.

A third clocker who was working for Pimlico at the time, E.T. McClean, caught Secretariat crossing the finish line in 1:54⅖. Two days after the race, Pimlico officials acknowledged that the electronic timer had malfunctioned, but they were unwilling to accept the *Daily Racing Form*'s insistence on a new stakes record. McClean's result became the official time for the 1973 Preakness, although questions about Secretariat's time lingered.

Challenges to Secretariat's "official" Preakness time have been considered by the Maryland Racing Commission on three occasions.

The first came in 1973, when a broadcast on CBS television (the network that televised the Triple Crown races that year) suggested that Secretariat actually had beaten Cañonero II's track record. The commission declined to change the stakes record, relying on a racing rule dictating that the time recorded by the track clocker would stand as the official time for any race when there was a question about the electronic equipment.

The second challenge, informally raised by Pimlico owner Joe De Francis, occurred during the late 1990s. Although the timing rule had been changed to allow revisions based on any "method considered reliable and accurate," the commission determined that there was not sufficient evidence to warrant changing the official time.

Finally, in 2012, the commission bowed to a request from Penny Chenery, who raced Secretariat in her Meadow Stable colors, and voted unanimously that Secretariat's time for the 1971 Preakness Stakes was, in fact, 1:53. Leonard Lusky, head of a marketing company that handles licensing and publicity for Secretariat, organized the three-and-a-half-hour presentation to the commission. The commissioners heard testimony from seven witnesses and watched a rerun of Secretariat's Preakness in a side-by-side comparison with two others, won by Tank's Prospect (1985) and Louis Quatorze (1996).

Both Tank's Prospect and Louis Quatorze won in what was assumed to be stakes record time, 1:53⅖. When the three recordings were viewed at the same time, however, Secretariat appeared to run marginally faster. This was sufficient evidence to convince the seven commissioners, and following a few minutes of deliberation, the result was announced. Almost forty years after the fact, by executive fiat, Secretariat became the "new" Preakness Stakes record holder.[94] The horse now holds the official records for all three Triple Crown races.

"Emotionally, for me, it doesn't do anything," Chenery said after the hearing. "I know how good he was, and his fans know how good he was; but for racing records, it's just best we have the right information."[95]

⸻•⸻

No one could doubt Cañonero II's versatility with two-thirds of the Triple Crown in the record books. The horse ran like completely different horses in the two races, coming from far off the pace to win the Kentucky Derby in a sluggish time and then pushing a confirmed speed horse for a mile before smashing a seventeen-year-old stakes record in the Preakness Stakes.

But why make such a radical change in race tactics that had worked so well the first time out?

The answer depended on whom you asked—and when. The answer also depended on who was acting as interpreter for the various members of Team Cañonero.

Through one interpreter, Gustavo Ávila said immediately after the race that he decided to send Cañonero II to the front because he did not want Eastern Fleet to set the pace without pressure from any other horse. Later, with the assistance of a different interpreter, Ávila said that he moved quickly with Cañonero II because he feared being blocked by other riders in the race if he employed the same come-from-behind tactics that had worked so well in the Derby. On a third occasion, the rider shared credit with Arias.

"Our strategy developed as the race was run," Ávila said. "I decided my horse could keep up with the leaders, so I sent him to the front. Arias had planned it that way, if it was possible."[96]

Juan Arias told reporters on Saturday that he wanted Ávila to go the front because he thought the track would be especially fast as it dried out after rain earlier in the week and that a fast track would benefit speed horses like Eastern Fleet and Executioner. He thought early speed might be too difficult to catch. Arias also was concerned about potential traffic problems.

"I decided to have Ávila try to go to the lead because of Cañonero's outside post position," the trainer told reporters assembled in the press box after the Preakness. "I didn't want him to be caught in the middle of horses. He can and has run on the lead or from off the pace in his past races. It makes no difference."[97]

The next day, Arias tacked in a different direction and reportedly said that Jim French's trainer, John Campo, really was behind the tactical change.

"Johnny Campo talked only about Jim French, Jim French," Arias explained, "so I told Ávila, 'You are near him in the post position, so get out of there quickly to get out of his way.' "[98]

A few days after the Preakness, in an interview with *Louisville Courier-Journal* and *Times* staff writer Ward Sinclair, who was fluent in Spanish and was one of the few reporters covering the Triple Crown who needed no interpreter, Pedro Baptista Sr. took credit for the winning tactics. The reason for the change, Don Pedro said, was to make a statement about Cañonero II.

"There was a lot of unfavorable comment, press, trainers and the like," Don Pedro told Sinclair. "To quiet these writers once and for all, I sent this horse out to head the field at the Preakness, to show just what he could do."[99]

The final analysis of what Arias called a "soft race" for Cañonero II came from Arias on the day before Cañonero II left Pimlico for Belmont Park.

"We thought that Jim French, on the outside, and Eastern Fleet, on the inside of us, would be the ones to beat," Arias said. "We wanted to get off quickly, to avoid being trapped. When Ávila found he was outrunning most of the others, he just let his horse run and then took hold of him on the backstretch. We think he could have gone by Eastern Fleet at any time."[100]

Even taking communication breakdowns into account, there was a nugget of truth in each of the explanations. Ávila was a skilled and astute rider who would be quick to take advantage of favorable circumstances as the race developed, and Cañonero II's stakes-record time affirmed Arias's conviction that the track would be lightning fast and that early speed would have an advantage.

Don Pedro's comment, however, was the most telling of all. He resented the cavalier attitude displayed toward his horse in Kentucky. A smashing win in the Preakness Stakes was the best way to thumb his nose at the people who had

Pedro Baptista Jr. hoists the replica of the Woodland Vase presented to the owner of the Preakenss Stakes winner. *Winants Brothers photo. Courtesy of* Blood-Horse.

ignored Cañonero II before the Kentucky Derby and who had refused to give the horse any credit afterward.

Juan Arias had taken the brunt of the criticism at Churchill Downs and Pimlico and like Don Pedro, the comments had hurt him deeply.

"I have a right to be taken seriously," he said after the Preakness, "and so do my horse and my jockey and my people. They say we are clowns. They say we are Indians because my horse gallops slowly, sometimes without a saddle. They come to look at my horse but turn away and wrinkle up their noses. Now I no longer have to justify myself. What can they say now?"[101]

With the first Triple Crown since Citation on the line at the Belmont Stakes in three weeks, only one question remained:

EIGHTH RACE **Pim 45516** **May 15, 1971**

1 3-16 MILES. (Nashua, May 28, 1955, $1{:}54\frac{3}{5}$, 3, 126.) Ninety-sixth running PREAKNESS. Scale weights. $150,000 added. 3-year-olds. By subscription of $100 each, this fee to accompany the nomination. $1,000 to pass the entry box, starters to pay $1,000 additional. All eligibility, entrance and starting fees to the winner, with $150,000 added, of which $30,000 to second, $15,000 to third and $7,500 to fourth. Weight, 126 lbs. A replica of the Woodlawn Vase will be presented to the winning owner and remain his or her personal property. Closed Monday, Feb. 15, 1971 with 179 nominations.
Value of race $189,900. Value to winner $137,400; second, $30,000; third, $15,000; fourth, $7,500.
Mutuel Pool, $736,768.

Index	Horses	Eq't A	Wt	PP	St	1/4	1/2	3/4	Str	Fin	Jockeys	Owners	Odds to $1
45409CD[1]	—Canonero II.	3	126	9	5	2^{h}	$2^{2\frac{1}{2}}$	2^{5}	1^{h}	$1^{1\frac{1}{2}}$	G Avila	E Caibett	3.40
45409CD[4]	—Eastern Fleet	b3	126	5	4	$1^{1\frac{1}{2}}$	1^{h}	1^{h}	2^{4}	$2^{4\frac{1}{2}}$	E Maple	Calumet Farm	6.40
45409CD[2]	—Jim French	b3	126	11	8	6^{2}	6^{h}	7^{1}	$4^{1\frac{1}{2}}$	3no	A C'dero Jr	F J Caldwell	2.40
45452Pim[1]	—Sound Off	b3	126	1	1	3^{1}	$4\frac{1}{2}$	$3\frac{1}{2}$	$3^{2\frac{1}{2}}$	$4\frac{1}{2}$	C Baltazar	G Ring	10.90
45409CD[3]	—Bold Reason	b3	126	7	6	9^{h}	9^{1}	$9\frac{1}{2}$	6^{3}	5^{6}	J Cruguet	W A Levin	12.40
45452Pim[2]	—Executioner	3	126	6	10	10^{h}	$8\frac{1}{2}$	$6^{1\frac{1}{2}}$	5^{h}	$6\frac{1}{2}$	J Vasquez	October House Farm	3.90
45453Pim[4]	—Royal J. D.	3	126	8	11	11	11	11	11	7no	E Belmonte	J M Davis	54.80
45409CD[6]	—Vegas Vic	b3	126	4	9	8^{h}	$7^{1\frac{1}{2}}$	$8^{1\frac{1}{2}}$	8^{h}	8^{h}	W Hartack	C Fritz	10.10
45409CD[13]	—Impetuosity	3	126	3	3	5^{2}	$5^{1\frac{1}{2}}$	$5\frac{1}{2}$	9^{h}	9^{1}	E Guerin	W P Rosso	17.20
45452Pim	—Spouting Horn	b3	126	10	7	$4\frac{1}{2}$	3^{2}	4^{h}	7^{1}	10^{nk}	J Kurtz	W D Fletcher	81.40
45452Pim[3]	—Limit to Reason	3	126	2	2	$7^{1\frac{1}{2}}$	10^{4}	10^{4}	10^{1}	11	J Velasquez	Brookmeade Stable	15.80

Time, $:23\frac{2}{5}$, :47, $1{:}10\frac{2}{5}$, 1:35, 1:54 (new track record). Track fast.

$2 Mutuel Prices:			
9-CANONERO II	8.80	6.20	4.00
5-EASTERN FLEET		8.20	5.20
11-JIM FRENCH			3.20

B. c, by Pretendre—Dixieland II., by Nantallah. Trainer, J. Arias. Bred by E. B. Benjamin (Ky.).

IN GATE—5:40. OFF AT 5:40½ EASTERN DAYLIGHT TIME. Start good for all but EASTERN FLEET and EXECUTIONER. Won driving.

CANONERO II., away in good order, quickly moved nearest the pace from the outside on the clubhouse turn, vied for the lead outside EASTERN FLEET to the upper stretch, gained the advantage a furlong out and drew clear in the final sixteenth under right-handed punishment. EASTERN FLEET broke to the outside at the start, bumped badly with EXECUTIONER, recovered quickly to gain the lead before the clubhouse turn and drew clear, vied for the lead with CANONERO II. thereafter to the final sixteenth, then weakened slightly. JIM FRENCH raced within striking distance of the early leaders, responded between horses in the stretch but could not threaten the leaders in the final furlong. SOUND OFF, away fast and forwardly placed for a half mile, continued willingly but could not gain ground thereafter. BOLD REASON, steadied on horses' heels on the clubhouse turn, dropped back and offered only a mild rally outside horses in the final quarter mile. EXECUTIONER broke to the inside, bumped solidly with EASTERN FLEET, was slow to recover and passed only tired horses in the final quarter mile. ROYAL J D lacked early speed and never reached contention. VEGAS VIC was never prominent with an even effort. IMPETUOSITY, forwardly placed early, saved ground much of the trip but lacked a strong finish. SPOUTING HORN had early speed but failed to stay. LIMIT TO REASON was always outrun in a dull effort. Following the running the stewards called an "inquiry," but allowed the original finish to stand.

Official chart of the 1971 Preakness Stakes. *Copyright circa 2013 by Daily Racing Form, LLC and Equibase Company. Reprinted with permission of the copyright owner.*

Which version of Cañonero II would show up in New York—the stayer or the sprinter?

Chapter 5

DÉJÀ VU ALL OVER AGAIN[102]

The year 1923 marked one of eleven times in which the Preakness Stakes was run before the Kentucky Derby.[103] Horses traveled cross-country by train in the 1920s, and among the first shipment of Thoroughbreds from Baltimore arriving in Louisville for the Derby that year was the winner of the Preakness: Vigil.

The *New York Times* noted the train's arrival in Kentucky:

"Thomas J. Healey had Walter J. Salmon Jr.'s Preakness winner, Vigil, and his owner wired today to say that he would be here Friday to see his colt try to capture his second classic in the triple crown of the American turf."[104]

Champion Zev ran twelfth in the Preakness that year, more than twenty-five lengths behind Vigil, and trainer Sam Hildreth initially decided not to run him in the Derby a week later. Hildreth reconsidered at the last minute, entered Zev and the colt won the Derby at odds of more than twenty to one. Vigil finished third.

More interesting than the 1923 Derby itself was the *New York Times* article about the early arrivals. It was one of the first occasions—maybe the very first—when the Derby, Preakness and Belmont were linked together with specific reference to a "triple crown."[105] The author of the *Times* article was not identified, and the genesis of referring to a "Triple Crown" series of specific races was not explored. There was little precedent for the idea at the time. Only Sir Barton, in 1919, had managed to string together victories in the Derby, Preakness and Belmont. The Triple Crown was a revolutionary idea that hardly anyone noticed, at least not for a few years.

Charles Hatton, veteran columnist for *Daily Racing Form*, generally is credited with popularizing the notion of a "Triple Crown" after Gallant Fox swept the series of races in 1930. In the years since, the Triple Crown has become one of the most elusive goals in sports. Only eleven three-year-olds have managed the feat: Sir Barton (1919), Gallant Fox (1930), Omaha (1935), War Admiral (1937), Whirlaway (1941), Count Fleet (1943), Assault (1946), Citation (1948), Secretariat (1973), Seattle Slew (1977) and Affirmed (1978).

As the series of races assumed a life of its own over the years, pursuit of the Triple Crown took on aspects of a mythic quest for owners, trainers and jockeys. There was enormous pressure to perform whenever a horse came to the Belmont Stakes with a chance to sweep the series. As the drought of Triple Crown winners following Citation lengthened throughout the 1950s and 1960s, people began to wonder whether there ever would be another. For some three-year-olds, the Triple Crown became a war of attrition.

Tim Tam in 1958 was the first horse since Citation to have a shot at the Triple Crown. The Calumet colt broke down in the stretch but still finished a game second to Cavan. Dr. Jacques Jenney, the pioneering orthopedic surgeon who led the team that saved the life of Hoist the Flag, was Tim Tam's veterinarian.

Three years later, Carry Back ran a lackluster seventh in Sherluck's Belmont, an effort that kept him away from the races until the fall. Champion Northern Dancer got close to the lead in the 1964 Belmont but wound up third behind Quadrangle and Roman Brother. Northern Dancer apparently came out of the Triple Crown grind in decent shape and won the Queen's Plate by seven and a half lengths in the horse's next—and final—start.

Kauai King was favored for the 1966 Belmont Stakes after winning the Derby and Preakness, but the horse finished fourth behind Amberoid. Questions about whether Kauai King or Buckpasser was the better three-year-old that year were answered in the Arlington Classic. Buckpasser won, the fifth consecutive win in what would become a fifteen-race string of victories extending from February 1966 until the upset in the Brooklyn Handicap fifteen months later. Kauai King broke down in the Arlington Classic and was retired. Buckpasser missed all three Triple Crown races due to an injury but was named Horse of the Year and champion of the division nevertheless.

Horse of the Year Dr. Fager, like Buckpasser, was spared the pressure and hype that accompanies every good horse during a Triple Crown campaign because of injury. The horse's trainer, John Nerud, was convinced that missing the Triple Crown races ultimately worked to Dr. Fager's benefit.[106] In 1968, as a four-year-old, Dr. Fager was named Horse of the Year and champion in the handicap, sprint and grass divisions.

Calumet Farm's Forward Pass would have had a dubious claim to a Triple Crown had the horse won the 1968 Belmont Stakes, but he finished second to Stage Door Johnny, the year's champion three-year-old male. Forward Pass was a well-beaten second behind Dancer's Image in the Kentucky Derby, but the winner tested positive for phenylbutazone, a painkiller prohibited under Kentucky's Rules of Racing. When Forward Pass won the Preakness by actually crossing the finish line in first place, the official order of finish for the Derby still was in dispute and would remain in limbo for years. Dancer's Image eventually was disqualified and placed last. Stage Door Johnny's win over Forward Pass in the Belmont eliminated the awkward situation of listing Forward Pass as a Triple Crown winner with an asterisk by the name.[107]

And then there was Majestic Prince, a brilliant colt whose Triple Crown campaign in 1969 proved that having a seemingly invincible horse can be both a blessing and a curse.

Canadian oilman Frank McMahon bought Majestic Prince as a yearling from breeder Leslie Combs II at the 1967 Keeneland summer yearling sale. Well-bred (Raise a Native–Gay Hostess, by Royal Charger) and handsome, Majestic Prince was the most expensive yearling sold at auction that year, going for $250,000. McMahon had a distinct advantage in the bidding war, although no one knew it at the time. He owned a half interest in Majestic Prince's dam and was bidding for the colt with fifty-cent dollars.[108]

McMahon turned Majestic Prince over to jockey-turned-trainer John Longden, who recognized that he had something special in the striking chestnut colt. Longden took his time with Majestic Prince, picked his races carefully and shipped to Churchill Downs for the Derby with a colt boasting a perfect record. Majestic Prince held off Arts and Letters by a neck in the Derby and by a head in the Preakness Stakes, and the horse was a clear favorite to become the first undefeated Triple Crown winner in the Belmont Stakes.

Then John Longden did the unthinkable.

"Boys, I'm taking him home," Longden announced to the press the day after the Preakness. With a Triple Crown on the line, Longden was going back to California. Majestic Prince was tired from a demanding schedule—the Belmont would be the colt's tenth start in a little over six months—and he had lost weight. It could not have been a decision that Longden made lightly. He already had the distinction of being the only person to both ride and train a Kentucky Derby winner and now he would be giving up the chance to become the only person to ride and train the winner of a Triple Crown.

Leslie Combs II, who expected to stand Majestic Prince at his Spendthrift Farm following the horse's retirement, agreed with Longden.

"He's raced a lot, and he's worked hard between his races," Combs said. "He won't run in the Belmont if I have anything to do with it."

McMahon concurred with the decision at first, albeit reluctantly, but then changed his mind in the face of growing criticism. Reporters searched for another occasion when the owner of a Derby and Preakness winner had voluntarily passed up the Belmont Stakes and could find none. It was not fair to the fans, the critics said, or to racing, or even to the horse to hold Majestic Prince out of the Belmont Stakes, at least if the horse was sound and not just tired. Majestic Prince was sound, McMahon proclaimed, and he would run in the Belmont after all.

"If he loses, so what?"[109]

Majestic Prince ran and lost. Arts and Letters finally turned the tables on his Derby and Preakness rival, winning easily by five and a half lengths. Majestic Prince never raced again, and championship honors at year's end went to Arts and Letters.

There was another Triple Crown on the line two years later with a similar story line.

Like Majestic Prince, Cañonero II was a wildly popular horse that might not be at his best, and there was disagreement about what to do, either run in the Belmont Stakes or sit it out for the horse's sake and abandon any chance of sweeping the Triple Crown. It was the Majestic Prince saga reimagined with an unwieldy cast of characters that included the Baptista family, Juan Arias, Gustavo Ávila, veterinarians from the United States and Venezuela, the press, potential buyers who would pay more for a Triple Crown winner than a nonstarter or an also-ran, track officials who needed Cañonero II in the race for a record crowd and betting handle, assorted advisors and an incalculable number of fans in this country and in Venezuela.

Caught in the maelstrom, like Majestic Prince in 1969, was Cañonero II.

— • —

Juan Arias arrived at Belmont Park on Thursday after the Preakness with Cañonero II in tow and a healthy dose of optimism.

Cañonero II at Belmont Park. *Courtesy of* Blood-Horse.

"He is a horse of destiny," Arias said. "He is the champion of all the people—black and white, rich and poor, American and Venezuelan, everyone."

It must have seemed to Arias as if the "people" had come to Barn 7A to take possession of their horse in the days leading up to the Belmont Stakes. Arias had trained Cañonero II to suit himself prior to the Kentucky Derby, when no one paid any attention to the horse other than to poke fun at the trainer's unconventional methods. Two weeks later at Pimlico, with a somewhat more attentive cadre of reporters and photographers hanging around the Preakness barn, Arias still managed to maintain the same light training schedule for Cañonero II. Now, though, with the stakes even higher, reporters and rumors dogged Arias at every turn.

To the surprise of most observers who thought Arias was doing everything wrong, Cañonero II managed to win the Derby and Preakness off a series of long, slow gallops and a couple of painfully slow workouts— plus one serious speed move that no one knew about. Arias gamely tried to approach the Belmont Stakes in the same low-key fashion.

After Cañonero II got a first taste of the Belmont racing strip, a slow one-and-a-half-mile gallop on May 21, Arias announced that, as before, he planned no traditional speed workouts for the colt:

"There will be no works per se," Arias told reporters. "We'll just gallop him, which is his regular way of training. If I feel that he needs a faster work, I will give it to him, but this is not usual."

Gustavo Ávila, who rode Cañonero II that morning before heading back to Venezuela for a few days, said that the colt liked the track at Belmont Park.

"He handled the track very well," the jockey said. "It seemed deeper than either Churchill Downs or Pimlico, but it was a track he appeared to like. He was alert and curious, which is the tip-off that he likes the track."[110]

Arias was true to his word. Cañonero II had a first timed workout on May 26, and like the colt's previous "official" workouts at Churchill Downs and at Pimlico, it was painfully slow: four furlongs in 0:53⅗. Jim French also worked four furlongs that morning, going in 0:46⅕, almost seven seconds faster than Cañonero II. Another Belmont horse, Good Behaving, clocked 0:49. Good Behaving was a multiple stakes winner in New York, but the horse had not been entered in any of the Triple Crown races. His owner, Neil Hellman, supplemented the colt for the Belmont, where he would run as an entry with Jim French, giving John Campo an opportunity to double-team Cañonero II.

Supremely confident in public, Arias nevertheless harbored doubts about whether Cañonero II could be ready for the most difficult challenge of the horse's life.

The horse had weathered assorted physical problems at Churchill Downs and at Pimlico, but Arias had a new set of worries prior to the Belmont Stakes. First was a skin rash spreading on the right side of Cañonero II's body. A minor concern before the Preakness, when it first appeared, the rash was getting worse every day. Dr. William O. Reed, a veterinarian called in to treat the rash, said that the skin condition was of "no consequence. It is a fungus infection, and we have treated it with medications. It should not bother him at all. It started at Pimlico and has spread around some here." The rash, Dr. Reed added, "would not keep him out of the race. You would not notice it at all if it were not for the medication."[111]

Public statements aside, the skin condition afflicting Cañonero II probably was more serious that anyone associated with the colt would admit. E. Barry Ryan, a prominent trainer who had stalls in the same barn where Cañonero II was stabled, thought the rash was compromising the colt's training.

Ryan told *Daily Racing Form* columnist Teddy Cox:

Well, first of all, I'm not fixin' to tell anyone how to train his horse, and I certainly don't care to put the knock on a colt that's done so well in the Derby and Preakness. But if this were my horse, there would be absolutely no chance for him to compete in the Belmont. Of course, such skin conditions respond to treatment in various ways. But in my experience, I've never had any luck in trying to train horses with this type of condition. The eruptions are in a bad spot, too, and seem to be spreading throughout his body.

It is impossible to tighten a saddle girth without causing pain and irritation. Of course, they have a way of training their horses in South America without girths, but this condition is so bad that I can't see how training can do anything but further irritate the condition.[112]

Everyone in the Cañonero II camp had been cooperative with reporters and talkative to a fault in Louisville and again in Baltimore. As rumors of Cañonero II's skin rash and other ailments began to swirl around the Belmont Park backstretch, however, people became testy and reticent.

"If we have anything to say, you will hear about it in a few days," a spokesman for Team Cañonero said in response to a question about the colt.[113]

Adding to the growing confusion about Cañonero II's physical condition, rumors began to circulate that the colt had developed a bad case of thrush in a hind foot. Thrush is an infection of the frog tissue on the underside of a horse's hoof that produces a foul odor and a black discharge. The condition usually is not serious and generally responds well to treatment, which typically involves trimming away the infected tissue and medicating the affected area for several days.[114]

Dr. Jose Hernandez-Rosal, Cañonero II's regular veterinarian in Venezuela, was on hand for the Belmont. He announced that "the skin rash is of no consequence and is clearing up. The foot infection is minor and has responded to treatment."[115]

Arias steadfastly maintained that Cañonero II was a "fit horse,"[116] but owners and trainers who had planned to pass up a meeting with the Derby and Preakness winner in the Belmont Stakes wondered about that and began to reconsider. What was expected to be a small field of a half dozen or so eventually would swell to thirteen horses, the largest field for the Belmont since 1954, and one of the largest ever. The only time that a Belmont Stakes attracted fourteen horses was the inaugural running in 1875, when Calvin defeated Kentucky Derby winner Aristides.

Around the time that rumors of a serious case of thrush began to surface, Arias called in a farrier to fit Cañonero II with a new set of racing plates and to treat the infection. Arias spoke no English, the farrier spoke no Spanish and the trainer had difficulty explaining how he wanted the colt reshod. Cañonero II was in pain after the infected part of the frog was pared away and missed two days of training while recovering.[117] The unanticipated break in Cañonero II's training disappointed several hundred early bird spectators to the track who expected to see the Derby and Preakness winner under tack and once again raised questions about whether Cañonero II could be ready for the Belmont Stakes.

Arias deflected the question and joked about the missed training time—"One does not run in a brand new pair of shoes"[118]—and said that the unexpected change in schedule would not bother Cañonero II: "You will remember that at Pimlico, before the Preakness, he also missed a day of training. Still, he ran well."[119]

After two days off, Cañonero II was sound and back in training. On Sunday, May 30, with just six days remaining before the Belmont Stakes, the horse galloped a slow two and a half miles over the turf course, with 135-pound exercise rider Earl Whye substituting for Gustavo Ávila. Whye rode with only a saddle pad, no saddle or stirrups, and it was all he could do to keep a rank Cañonero II from running away with him.

"My hands hurt from trying to hold him back," Whye said of the gallop. "This horse wanted to run."[120]

Arias once again affirmed that Cañonero II was fit and would be ready for the Belmont Stakes. The rumor mill suggested that Arias worked Cañonero II on grass because of the thrush infection; Arias responded that he had been misquoted in various news reports and press releases about Cañonero II even having thrush.

"I never said that," Arias insisted with Dr. José Almonar translating for reporters.

Speaking on his own accord, Dr. Almonar staunchly defended Arias.

"It is wrong. He never said anything about an infection…and there is no thrush."

"No thrush, no thrush," Arias reiterated with passion in his voice, this time without needing anyone to translate for him. A minor hoof problem had developed while Cañonero II was held in quarantine in Florida, Arias explained, but it had been treated successfully and no longer was a concern. "No thrush," he said again for emphasis.[121] Just who Arias was trying to convince, whether it was the reporters hanging around the barn, the public or himself, was not at all clear. What was becoming abundantly clear, though, was that everyone associated with Cañonero II had closed ranks in an effort to deflect any criticism aimed at Arias or the colt.

Reputation mattered because Cañonero II was for sale. Pedro Baptista Sr. confirmed that he had received offers to buy Cañonero II from eight different groups in the United States, Venezuela, England and Japan. There had been offers after the Preakness as well, but Don Pedro said that a sense of national pride kept him from considering them at that time.

"I owe it to my people in Venezuela that Cañonero II have his chance to win the Triple Crown in the colors of my country, where he has become a national hero."[122] That almost did not happen, even without a prerace sale that would have transferred ownership of Cañonero II to someone else. The solid brown silks and cap that Cañonero II carried without complaint from anyone in the Derby and Preakness actually were registered with the Jockey Club in the name of Calvin M.B. Brown. It took a last-minute dispensation from the Jockey Club to allow Cañonero II to carry those colors in the Belmont Stakes.

Cañonero II stayed on the turf course for Monday exercise and then returned to the main track for a one-and-a-half-mile gallop with Gustavo Ávila in the saddle on Tuesday. The colt had a second, and last, serious workout on Wednesday. Ávila galloped Cañonero II slowly once around the one-and-a-half-mile main track, and then on his second circuit, he asked the colt for some speed at the five-furlong pole. Cañonero's time for five furlongs, 1:04, was, as always, slow by conventional standards. Arias, as always, was satisfied.

"My horse is okay, just fine," the trainer said. "I've beaten most of the others, and there is no reason why I can't beat them again."[123]

Arias was overstating his case a bit when he said that Cañonero II already had beaten "most" of the horses he would face in the Belmont. Actually, only four of Cañonero II's twelve rivals had run in the Derby or Preakness. There was Jim French and Bold Reason, of course, veterans of both classics; Twist the Axe, tenth in the Kentucky Derby; and Royal JD, seventh in the Preakness Stakes.

Among the mostly overlooked "others" was October House Farm's Pass Catcher, a lightly raced son of All Hands that had never won a stakes race but was coming into the Belmont off a strong second-place finish in the Jersey Derby just five days earlier. Pass Catcher was a last-minute addition to the Belmont field. The horse had filled the role of backup to another of owner Peter Kissell's three-year-olds, Executioner, for most of the year, but the first-stringer was sore after being bumped hard by Eastern Fleet at the start of the Preakness.

Kissell originally planned to run Pass Catcher in the Jersey Derby and Executioner in the Belmont Stakes, but Executioner's injury in the Preakness forced a change of plans.

"With Executioner out," Kissell said, "I thought last week, 'Oh, what the hell, Pass Catcher is the only other three-year-old I have, so we might as well run him in the Belmont.'"[124]

Using the Jersey Derby as a prep race for the Belmont Stakes was familiar ground for trainer Eddie Yowell. Six years earlier, when Belmont Park was being rebuilt and the Belmont Stakes was run at Aqueduct, Yowell won the race with Jersey Derby winner Hail to All, defeating Preakness Stakes winner and eventual three-year-old champion Tom Rolfe in the process. In other years, Yowell's earlier success with Hail to All might have attracted some support from bettors looking for a trainer with a winning pattern, but 1971 had become the year of Cañonero II. Pass Catcher started at odds of almost thirty-five to one.

Injuries, those that were public knowledge and those that were not, shaped the field for the Belmont Stakes.

Questions about Cañonero II's physical condition—the skin rash that either was or was not serious, the often-denied thrush, the interrupted training, all of which had been received attention in the media—did little to dampen enthusiasm for the colt's chances to sweep the Triple Crown.

A last-minute plea to scratch Cañonero II for the good of the horse and everyone else in *Sports Illustrated* fell on deaf ears:

> *Perhaps sometime before the Belmont this Saturday, Cañonero II's handlers will forget false national pride and scratch the horse. We hope so. He is in bad shape and has been for a week. He has a skin disease, his ankles are burned behind (that is, he has "run down" on Belmont's deep track), and he has been suffering from thrush, a painful fungus infection like athlete's foot, found underneath the frog of the hoof (his right hind one).*
>
> *If there were not the pressure to run for the greater glory of Venezuela and the greater handle of Belmont, Cañonero would have been scratched long ago and saved to race when he is fit. To pretend that he is a miracle horse with recuperative powers to match his heart is a whimsy that can only hurt the colt, his reputation, and the people—bettors and laymen alike—who have come to love him.*[125]

No matter how well-intentioned they might have been, the editors of *Sports Illustrated*, like Don Quixote, were tilting at windmills. There was too much at stake—the Triple Crown, the hefty weight of public opinion, money, reputations, the pride of a nation—to quit now. There was no way that Cañonero II was going to be scratched.

A record crowd of 82,694 turned out for the Belmont Stakes on a perfect early summer day. It was the largest number of fans ever to watch a Thoroughbred race in New York, and judging by the decibels of their cheering, the fluttering Venezuelan flags and the Latin music, everyone was there to see Cañonero II. They showed their support at the betting windows, setting wagering records both at Belmont Park and at off-track parlors scattered across the city, and the "people's horse" went to the post as the odds-on favorite. The entry of Jim French and Good Behaving (at odds of nearly four to one) and Purse Finder (seven to one) were the only other horses with any significant support from the bettors.

Pass Catcher, meanwhile, had his own physical problems and was a questionable starter almost up to post time for the Belmont. Yowell had not made a final decision about running Pass Catcher until the last possible moment to allow time to evaluate the colt's condition after a hard-fought race in the Jersey Derby earlier in the week. The decision to run or not became even more difficult on Belmont Day. When Yowell

There was a strong Venezuelan contingent supporting Cañonero II in the bid for the Triple Crown. *Courtesy of* Blood-Horse.

arrived at the track from his home in New Jersey early on the morning of the race, he learned that Pass Catcher had become cast in his stall during the night and had rapped an ankle trying to get to his feet.

The ankle was swollen, but Yowell hoped that the injury was not serious. He conferred with Dr. Manual A. Gilman, track veterinarian for the New York Racing Association. Dr. Gilman was responsible for examining the day's starters and scratching any horse that appeared lame. He told Yowell that he would allow Pass Catcher to race, but that the final decision was up to the trainer.

For Walter Blum, the veteran jockey who had ridden Pass Catcher in his last three races, the decision was an easy one. Although Bold Reasoning had beaten Pass Catcher by a half length in the Jersey Derby, Blum was convinced that the colt was improving and was ready for a big race. He urged Yowell to give the colt a chance in the Belmont.

"I figured, you only have a shot at the Belmont once a year, so I sent him out," Yowell said.[126]

Yowell did not have much to say to Blum in the paddock before the Belmont.

"He knew that I knew Pass Catcher and that Pass Catcher knew me," Blum recalled years later. "He said, 'The horse to beat is Cañonero II. Keep an eye on him. Don't let him get away from you. Ride him the best you can. Get a good position. When you ask him, you know he's going to answer.'"[127]

Breaking from post position No. 7, Gustavo Ávila hustled Cañonero II to the front just as he had done in the Preakness and the colt had the lead as the horses galloped into the first turn. Blum had Pass Catcher exactly where he wanted to be, running in second place on the rail, going easily and tracking Cañonero II stride for stride. As the field straightened into the backstretch, Cañonero II drew clear by two lengths: "Moving down the backstretch and Cañonero's going to make them catch him today."

Catch him they did.

With a mile still to run, Cañonero II was in front by two and a half lengths, and the colt looked poised to become the first Triple Crown winner since Citation. Bold Reason, Pass Catcher and Twist the Axe were tightly bunched behind Cañonero II, but were in danger of losing touch with the leader. No other horse was close.

Driving between Cañonero II and the rail, Twist the Axe was the first to make a bid to catch the favorite. He closed the gap to a half-length, then to a

Cañonero II already had a clear lead with one and one-quarter miles to go in the Belmont Stakes. *Courtesy of* Blood-Horse.

With seven furlongs left to run, Cañonero II was still in front, but Twist the Axe, Bold Reason and Pass Catcher were all within striking distance. *Winants Brothers photo. Courtesy of* Blood-Horse.

head, but could get no closer. Bold Reason was a length farther back in third. "These two are now drawing up to Cañonero. He has not been extended at this point, just galloped along the backstretch. In fourth still is Pass Catcher."

Edward L. Bowen, managing editor of *Blood-Horse* magazine, was watching the race unfold from a high perch atop the Belmont Park grandstand. Next to him was veteran equine photographer Peter Winants, who was shooting sequence photographs of the race for the magazine. Bowen still remembers the chants of "Can-yon-na-ro," "Can-yon-na-ro" echoing up from the crowd packing the grandstand several levels below him, and the voice of Winants assessing the race: "not today," click; "not today," click; "not today," click.

Cañonero II finally put a tiring Twist the Axe away on the final turn, but now there was a new challenger. Walter Blum had Pass Catcher moving fastest of all on the outside, and he caught Cañonero II midway through the turn. "I believe Pass Catcher has taken over the lead. Yes, he has as they come to the quarter pole."

Pass Catcher quickly drew away to a five-length lead under a strong-hand ride from Blum. The rider did not need his whip, which was good because he no longer had one:

> *I hit him three or four times on the right side and opened up about two lengths. I hit him two or three more times on the left side. He was about three lengths in front coming to the quarter pole when I suddenly lost my*

Near the finish, Pass Catcher drew away from a tiring Cañonero II. Jim French (on the rail) and Bold Reason (on the outside) also passed Cañonero II to finish second and third. *Winants Brothers photo. Courtesy of* Blood-Horse.

whip. I didn't have to hit him a lot anyway, just give him the message that it was time to go, but I didn't want to finish the race without it.

I was embarrassed that I dropped the whip. I didn't say anything about it, the trainer didn't say anything, but the next day in the paper, the middle of the Daily News, *was a picture of me reaching for my whip in mid-air. So I had to admit that I did drop the whip.*[128]

Losing the whip did not matter. Cañonero II was finished, and a late charge from fast-closing Jim French fell short. "Jim French is picking up

Belmont Stakes winner Pass Catcher, a longshot at odds of thirty-five to one. *Courtesy of* Blood-Horse.

ground, he's moving fast, but at the wire, at the wire, at the wire it's Pass Catcher the winner."

Reliable Jim French caught Pass Catcher just past the finish line and would have won the race if the Belmont Stakes had been run at one and a half miles plus a half dozen or so strides. Bold Reason finished third, a neck in front of a tired Cañonero II. Eddie Belmonte, rider of Twist the Axe, claimed foul against the winner and the favorite for interference on the final turn, but the order of finish stood. The winner's time for one and a half miles was 2:30⅗, three and four-fifths seconds slower than the track record set by Gallant Man in 1957.

Standing in front of Cañonero II's stall on the morning after the Belmont Stakes, Arias candidly admitted what everyone associated with the horse had been denying for days: the colt simply was not ready for the demanding one-and-a-half-mile race.

Assisted with translation by Dr. José Almenar, Arias told Herb Goldstein of *Daily Racing Form* that he saddled Cañonero II "with a tear in my eye on Saturday. The days he lost in training cost him. He did not go to the track on Friday and Saturday the week before the Belmont. I wanted to work him a mile and an eighth that Saturday, and missing that work may have been the difference."[129]

Gustavo Ávila had come to the same conclusion the day before when he was interviewed after the Belmont Stakes.

"I have to believe that the two days of inactivity last week hurt him," Avila said. "He was going along well, but he tired in the stretch. I still think he's capable of running a mile and a half and winning at that distance. He came back sound, and he's a healthy horse. He simply tired."[130]

Arias also confirmed that the thrush infection in Cañonero II's right hind foot was more serious than ever reported.

"He had that terrible infection in his right hind foot when we arrived here from Pimlico," the trainer said. "We didn't know what it was at first, but when we pulled off his shoe, we found the trouble. It was so bad that we considered withdrawing him from the race, but his leg responded to treatment and we decided to run. But he just wasn't ready."[131]

A few days after the Belmont Stakes, an unidentified spokesman for the Baptista family suggested that Cañonero II's thrush infection might have started while the colt was held in quarantine in Miami prior to the Kentucky Derby.[132] That speculation makes some sense. Thrush often is associated with poor hygiene, and it is reasonable to question how often—or if—Cañonero II's stall was adequately cleaned while the horse was cooped up in a quarantine stall for four days.

The postrace admissions made by Arias and Ávila about the cumulative effects of Cañonero II's missed training time and the colt's ailments were welcome because they helped set the story straight, but they also created an apparent contradiction. If Cañonero II actually thrived on long gallops and little speed work, as Arias said of Cañonero II's preparation for the Kentucky Derby and Preakness Stakes, why did training disruptions matter so much

EIGHTH RACE Bel 45744 June 5, 1971

1 1-2 MILES. (Gallant Man, June 15, 1957, 2:26⅗, 3, 126.) One hundred third running BELMONT. Scale weights. $125,000 added. 3-year-olds. By subscription of $100 each, to accompany the nomination. Supplementary nominations may be made by Wednesday, June 2, by the payment of an eligibility fee of $5,000. $250 to pass the entry box and $1,000 additional to start, with $125,000 added. The added money and all fees to be divided 60 per cent to the winner. 22 per cent to second, 12 per cent to third and 6 per cent to fourth. Colts and geldings, 126 lbs.; fillies, 121 lbs. The winning owner will be presented with the August Belmont Memorial Cup, to be retained for one year, as well as a trophy for permanent possession and trophies will be presented to the winning trainer and jockey. (Closed Monday, Feb. 15, 1971 with 166 nominations and one supplementary.)
Value of race $162,850. Value to winner $97,710; second, $35,827; third, $19,542; fourth, $9,771.
Mutuel Pool, $1,120,843.

index	Horses	Eq't A	Wt	PP	¼	½	1	1¼	Str	Fin	Jockeys	Owners	Odds to $1
45633GS^{2}	—Pass Catcher	3	126	3	$2^{1/2}$	3^{h}	3^{1}	$1^{1\frac{1}{2}}$	1^{5}	$1^{3/4}$	W Blum	October House Farm	34.50
45516Pim^{3}	—Jim French	b3	126	10	$7^{1\frac{1}{2}}$	7^{h}	7^{2}	7^{5}	3^{h}	$2^{3\frac{1}{2}}$	A Cord'o Jr	F J Caldwell	a-3.50
45516Pim^{5}	—Bold Reason	b3	126	11	$3^{1\frac{1}{2}}$	2^{1}	$4^{1/2}$	4^{h}	4^{3}	3^{nk}	J Cruguet	W A Levin	12.70
45516Pim^{1}	—Canonero II.	3	126	7	1^{1}	$1^{2\frac{1}{2}}$	1^{h}	2^{2}	2^{1}	$4^{3/4}$	G Avila	E Caibett	.70
45434Bel^{4}	—Epic Journey	b3	126	1	13	13	11^{6}	$8^{1/2}$	8^{3}	$5^{1/2}$	J Velasq'ez	Ethel D Jacobs	48.70
45443Bel^{1}	—Purse Finder	b3	126	4	$6^{1/2}$	$6^{1/2}$	6^{3}	6^{1}	5^{h}	6^{3}	J Ruane	Briardale Farm	7.00
45416Bel^{1}	—Salem	3	126	9	$5^{1/2}$	$5^{1\frac{1}{2}}$	5^{3}	5^{1}	6^{1}	$7^{1\frac{1}{2}}$	J L Rotz	Christiana Stable	16.90
45633GS^{3}	—Twist the Axe	3	126	2	$4^{1\frac{1}{2}}$	4^{5}	2^{2}	$3^{1/2}$	$7^{1/2}$	$8^{1\frac{1}{2}}$	E Belmonte	Pastorale Stable	31.00
45461Aqu^{2}	—Highbinder	3	126	13	8^{h}	9^{4}	8^{1}	9^{2}	9^{2}	9^{2}	R Woodh'se	Tartan Stable	15.50
45570Pim^{2}	—Royal J. D.	3	126	12	10^{3}	10^{6}	$9^{1\frac{1}{2}}$	10^{10}	10^{14}	10^{16}	J Vasquez	J M Davis	108.10
45461Aqu^{4}	—(s) Good Behav'g	3	126	8	$11^{1/2}$	$12^{1\frac{1}{2}}$	13	13	13	$11^{1\frac{1}{2}}$	R Turcotte	N Hellman	a-3.50
45259GP.	—Adobe Ed	b3	126	5	9^{4}	$8^{1\frac{1}{2}}$	$10^{1/2}$	11^{3}	11^{h}	12^{nk}	M Venezia	J J Harris	245.80
45443Bel^{6}	—Sense A Fear	b3	126	6	12^{3}	$11^{1\frac{1}{2}}$	12^{2}	12^{5}	$12^{1/2}$	13	C Baltazar	S Stavro	171.20

a-Coupled: Jim French and Good Behaving. (s) Supplementary nomination.
Time, :24⅕, :48⅕, 1:12⅖, 1:37, 2:03, 2:30⅖ (crosswind in backstretch). Track fast.

$2 Mutuel Prices:			
4-PASS CATCHER	71.00	21.00	10.80
1A-JIM FRENCH (a-Entry)		3.60	2.80
10-BOLD REASON			4.80

B. c, by All Hands—La Grue, by Flaneur II. Trainer, E. Yowell. Bred by October House Farm (Ky.).
IN GATE—5:35. OFF AT 5:35 EASTERN DAYLIGHT TIME. Start good. Won driving.

PASS CATCHER, away alertly, was allowed to follow the leaders in hand, moved fast from the outside to catch CANONERO II. at the five-sixteenths pole, came over slightly while moving away to a clear advantage, continued to draw off after the rider lost his whip at the quarter-pole, settled into the stretch with a long lead and lasted over JIM FRENCH under a strong hand ride. The latter, unhurried while saving ground for a mile, moved through along the rail entering the stretch and finished strongly. BOLD REASON, sent into contention from the outside early, was well placed while saving ground to the far turn, came out for the drive and continued on with good courage. CANONERO II. took over racing into the first turn, made the pace while racing out from the rail, came in slightly when replaced by PASS CATCHER approaching the stretch and weakened during the drive. Foul claims against PASS CATCHER and CANONERO II. by the rider of TWIST THE AXE, for alleged interference coming to the quarter-pole, were not allowed. EPIC JOURNEY, outrun for a mile, rallied belatedly from the outside. PURSE FINDER lacked room along the inside at the first turn, recovered to race within easy striking distance to the stretch, but lacked the needed late response after coming out for the drive. SALEM made a bid from the outside rounding the far turn but was finished entering the stretch. TWIST THE AXE, away in good order, moved through along the rail to engage CANONERO II. midway along the backstretch, but lacked room along the inside while weakening approaching the stretch and gave way readily thereafter. HIGHBINDER was always outrun, as were ROYAL J. D. and GOOD BEHAVING. ADOBE ED tired. SENSE A FEAR showed nothing.

Exacta (4-1) Paid $275.60; Exacta Pool, $434,525.

Official chart of the 1971 Belmont Stakes. *Copyright circa 2013 by Daily Racing Form, LLC and Equibase Company. Reprinted with permission of the copyright owner.*

prior to the Belmont? Likely answers are that the conditions for the Belmont Stakes—the length of the race and a deep, sandy racing strip that was more tiring than the tracks in Kentucky and Maryland—demanded a horse that was fit and healthy. Cañonero II was neither going into the Belmont Stakes.

By race day, Arias and Cañonero II had become passengers on a speeding train inexorably bound by national pride and money toward the starting gate at Belmont Park. All Arias could do was his best with Cañonero II and hope that it would be good enough.

Pass Catcher's surprise victory and Cañonero II's disappointing loss silenced a nation's cheers in Venezuela.

"When we least expected it, Cañonero won the Derby for us," a Caracas sportscaster said. "When we were afraid to expect it, he won the Preakness. And when we fully expected a victory, he lost."[133]

Part 2

KING RANCH

Chapter 6
STYMIED

Cañonero II's game effort in the Belmont Stakes, despite being ill-prepared for the race's testing one and a half miles, drew praise from George Ryall, a writer who covered Thoroughbred racing for the *New Yorker* for more than a half century. From Man o' War in the 1920s through Triple Crown winners Secretariat, Seattle Slew and Affirmed in the 1970s, Ryall saw every great horse that raced. He did not think that Cañonero II received the credit he deserved:

> *He was in a state of almost complete exhaustion for days after the Belmont Stakes, and still walks in a gingerly way, with his head down. All the horsemen I've talked to about him agree that, considering his preparation in the fortnight before the race, he was hardly fit to run the mile and a half…For my part, I do not think that, in the circumstances, Cañonero II has had the praise he deserves for a gallant performance. He ran his heart out going as far as he could go—more than a mile at a smart pace. He gave everything he had, and no horse can do more than that. In my book, he's the hero of the 1971 Belmont Stakes.*[134]

Many of the multimillion-dollar offers to buy, lease or syndicate Cañonero II were contingent on a successful Triple Crown campaign. A moral victory in the race notwithstanding, those offers vanished after the Belmont. The only serious bid still on the table in June was from King Ranch owner Robert J. Kleberg Jr., who liked Cañonero II both as a racehorse and as a breeding stallion prospect.

From his first involvement with Thoroughbreds in the mid-1930s, when he was shopping for quarter horses and wound up with a Thoroughbred named Chicaro instead, until his death forty years later, Kleberg built King Ranch into a racing and breeding powerhouse. He bred and raced Triple Crown winner and Horse of the Year Assault, multiple champion Gallant Bloom, a second Kentucky Derby winner in Middleground and more than eighty other stakes winners. If there was a gap in Kleberg's impressive résumé, it was his inability to breed or develop a first-class sire.[135] Kleberg must have thought that a horse with a stayer's pedigree, the ability to win like a sprinter and the courage Cañonero II showed throughout the Triple Crown would fill the bill.

"I want that colt," he said,[136] and his interest never wavered.

Cañonero II caught Kleberg's eye at Churchill Downs, and negotiations to buy the colt continued through the Preakness and Belmont Stakes. Kleberg made an offer of $1.5 million before the Belmont Stakes, and the same offer from the King Ranch owner remained in play after the race. As on-again-off-again sale rumors made the rounds at Belmont Park, the only certainty was that Cañonero II's physical condition was a problem for any potential buyer.

The skin rash and the thrush still were there and apparently responding to treatment, but now Cañonero II had new ailments, an inflamed and seriously swollen right hock and a sore ankle. Whether Cañonero II injured the hock and ankle during the Belmont Stakes was the subject of much backstretch speculation, but King Ranch trainer William J. (Buddy) Hirsch acknowledged that it was impossible to know for certain when the colt was hurt.

Dr. Mark Gerard, who examined Cañonero II on behalf of Kleberg, checked the colt on Tuesday after the Belmont and then again on Wednesday. Cañonero II was racing sound on Tuesday, with no heat or inflammation in any of his joints, but the following day, the colt had the tender hock and a fever.[137]

In mid-June, Hirsch said that his boss still was interested in buying Cañonero II but that "the deal to buy this horse certainly has not been completed. That is not to say it will not be consummated at some future date. Right now, however, this horse certainly is not sound. Mr. Kleberg would like to race him in his colors, in the event he buys him, and then retire him to stud. But we are not going ahead under these conditions."[138]

Travel plans for Cañonero II's return to Caracas were made and cancelled several times as negotiations between Kleberg and bloodstock agent Luis Navas, who bought Cañonero II as a yearling for $1,200 and was representing the colt's owner, dragged on. By the end of June, although Cañonero II's physical problems still were unresolved, the deal with Kleberg was finalized for the original amount offered, $1.5 million.

Instead of traveling back to Venezuela, Cañonero II limped from Barn 7A to Barn 1 on the Belmont Park backstretch. The colt wound up in a stall next to Hoist the Flag, still recovering from the near-fatal breakdown he suffered a month before the Kentucky Derby. By late August, while Hoist the Flag still was confined to the stall, Cañonero II was out grazing for an hour each morning and afternoon and walking around the shedrow each day. [139] There was no possibility that Cañonero II would run again in 1971, but even that gloomy outlook proved to be overly optimistic. In fact, it took Buddy Hirsch almost a full year to get the Derby and Preakness winner sound enough to return to the races.

Although the horse had started only three times in the United States as a three-year-old and had won only twice, Cañonero II's victories in the Kentucky Derby and Preakness Stakes loomed large in the minds of voters who decided the year-end championships. The colt was named champion three-year-old male for 1971, and the Baptistas, Sr. and Jr., were on hand to accept the Eclipse Award trophy. It was the first year

Cañonero II received his share of get-well cards while he recuperated from the Triple Crown races. Mrs. Sandy Hirsch reads one of the cards to an interested Cañonero II outside the horse's stall in the King Ranch barn. *Courtesy of* Blood-Horse.

that the Thoroughbred Racing Associations, *Daily Racing Form* and the National Turf Writers Association combined their ballots to name unified champions in all divisions under the "Eclipse Award" banner. Prior to 1971, the TRA and *Daily Racing Form* had conducted separate polls to determine the best horses in their respective divisions each year, which occasionally resulted in co-champions.[140]

Don Pedro and Juan Arias parted company not on the best of terms after the Belmont Stakes, and Arias was conspicuously absent from the Eclipse Award ceremony. It was an unfortunate omission, one that denied Arias an opportunity to be recognized for the masterful, and wholly unexpected, training feat he accomplished during the Triple Crown.

Juan Arias was heartsick about the sale of Cañonero II. For a man who made his name and built his reputation training one very good horse, Arias was losing a significant part of his identity. The exploits of the Derby and Preakness winner had put money in Arias's pocket and elevated him to a position of prominence in the world he loved best, the world of Thoroughbred racing, and now the money and the fame were gone. Hardest for Arias to take, however, even considering that he was losing the best horse he would ever train, was the fact that he also was losing a friend in Cañonero II.

"It would be like getting married and then having your wife go away from you," he told reporters with the aid of an interpreter after the Preakness. "I'll be broken down if he is sold." Acknowledging that the decision to sell Cañonero II was owner Pedro Baptista Sr.'s and not his, Arias added philosophically, "He's the owner. I'm the professional man training the best I can. I hope he gets the best price he can."[141]

Arias must have wondered then, must wonder still, how to put a price on a horse like Cañonero II, how to put a price on a friend.

———•———

Buddy Hirsch faced a formidable task when he took over the conditioning of Cañonero II after the Belmont Stakes.

"We had to work on the hock—it was the size of a man's head—and give him a great deal of personal attention," Hirsch said.[142] "Personal attention" would prove to be an understatement.[143]

Cañonero II was grazed and walked by a groom through all of September, while Dr. Gerard tapped the colt's hock to remove fluid on a regular basis. Then Cañonero started walking under tack around the shedrow in October.

Cañonero II and King Ranch trainer William J. (Buddy) Hirsch. *Courtesy of* Blood-Horse.

Hirsch jogged Cañonero II on the main track at Belmont Park for the first time on October 12, and by mid-November, the horse was jogging three-quarters of a mile. The horse's training was sidetracked on November 25, when his right hind ankle filled and he came down with a cracked heel. The new ailments were the first of many future problems that would plague Cañonero II through the rest of the horse's career.

Hirsch left Cañonero II at Belmont Park to recuperate when he took the rest of the King Ranch horses to Saratoga in the summer. By December, when the stable shipped to California for the winter, Cañonero II went along. By that time, the horse had developed a fungus infection on his injured heel, was being treated for thrush again and his training regimen—if you could call it that—was reduced to walking. Hirsch started galloping Cañonero II after the first of the year, and on January 24, 1972, the horse breezed for the first time since a few days before the Belmont Stakes the year before—three furlongs in 0:36⅗. People turned out in droves to watch Cañonero II exercise in the mornings, because those workouts were the only opportunities for

West Coast fans to see the horse in action. The horse never was close to making a start during his months in California.

Cañonero II was making slow, but relatively steady, progress until early February, when his ankle filled again. Hirsch lost nine days' valuable training time while dealing with the ankle. Cañonero II finally managed several weeks of uninterrupted work in March and April, and by the time the horse was shipped back to New York, he was breezing three-quarters of a mile in 1:14.

Cañonero II made his first start in the King Ranch colors on May 20, 1972, in the seven-furlong Carter Handicap. Carrying 121 pounds, Cañonero II rallied from last place to finish second over a sloppy track. It seemed to be an auspicious return to the races after eleven months, but Cañonero II's form tapered off after the Carter. The horse had "run down"—scraped the back of his right hind ankle raw—in the Carter, and he had the same problem when he finished eighth in the Metropolitan Handicap nine days later. In his next two starts, both on grass, Cañonero II finished sixth in allowance company and ninth in the Tidal Handicap.

Two weeks later, at Saratoga Race Course, *Blood-Horse* editor Kent Hollingsworth happened upon Cañonero II in the paddock prior to a $15,000 allowance race for nonwinners of $6,800 three times in 1971 and 1972.

"It seemed odd," Hollingsworth wrote, "that last year's champion would be eligible for such an event, but there was Cañonero II, an honest champion as he proved in the Kentucky Derby and Preakness, a horse of rare courage as he showed in the Belmont."[144]

Cañonero II ran closer to the pace than usual that August afternoon and finished second, but the horse still was six lengths behind Onion. A year later, in Saratoga's Whitney Handicap, Onion would upset Horse of the Year and Triple Crown winner Secretariat.

Kleberg, meanwhile, never lost faith.

"I still believe I've never seen a better-looking horse," he said after the Metropolitan. "I'd like to win one good race with him—say the Suburban on July 22—and then syndicate him for stud duty."[145] Cañonero II did not make the Suburban, won by Hitchcock, instead finishing sixth in an allowance race around the same time.

Speculation at the time was that Cañonero II would be syndicated for $50,000 a share to stand at A.B. Hancock Jr.'s Claiborne Farm when the horse's racing days were over. At that price, Kleberg would recoup Cañonero II's purchase price if there were buyers for thirty-two shares. Hancock suggested that the price was optimistic.

"It would be hard to get that for him right now," Hancock said. "His pedigree is against him. It would help if he'd won in New York during his career. It would help tremendously if he won the Suburban, and it would be a lot easier if he'd won the 1971 Belmont Stakes instead of the Preakness. But we'll do our best."[146]

———•———

Always nervous and high-strung, traits that accounted for the blindfolded starts in the Kentucky Derby and Belmont Stakes, Cañonero II became rank and tried to bear out when the horse returned to the races as a four-year-old. Hirsch fiddled with the tack, adding and removing blinkers and trying a softer snaffle bit with prongs, and he switched exercise riders until he found Eddie Deas. A rider with a reputation for handling difficult horses, Deas proved to be a good match for Cañonero II.

"Eddie started working with Cañonero," Hirsch told *Daily Racing Form*. "At first, the colt was rank and rough as usual. He had been fighting other exercise boys so much this year that he'd often come back with his mouth bleeding. After a few days with Eddie he began to act more kindly…The secret was to put it all together. That is, the new exercise boy, the new bit, and the new type of blinker."

Deas told *Daily Racing Form*:

> *Cañonero was a challenge. I've been on a lot of others like him, and I've managed to get along when others failed. The big secret is kindness and your ability to relate your feelings to the horse so he won't think you're cruel and that you're not on his back to force your will on him. The first morning I got on Cañonero, he fought back but I more or less let him have his way. He did not come back to the barn bleeding at the mouth. The next morning he was better, and he continued to become more relaxed.*

Deas was riding Cañonero II the same way that Juan Arias trained him, and the horse responded to the kinder, gentler treatment. Hirsch also discovered, as Arias had before him, that Cañonero II did not require frequent speed work.

"I didn't work him real fast all that time," Hirsch said. "I didn't want to overtrain him. He doesn't need it. He is a good doer—usually a strong horse as big as he is [16.2 hands] needs a little more training—but they are all different."

William J. (Buddy) Hirsch (walking) learned not to "overtrain" Cañonero II. *Courtesy of* Blood-Horse.

Hirsch found the final piece of the puzzle in a stack of fan mail addressed to Cañonero II and a suggestion from Robert Kleberg Jr. Armchair trainers had been writing to suggest that Hirsch bring Gustavo Ávila back from Venezuela to ride Cañonero II as a way to get the horse out of his slump. John L. Rotz had ridden the horse in his first four starts for King Ranch before Heliodoro Gustines took over. Cañonero II had run second twice, once for Rotz and once for Gustines, but neither jockey had been able to win a race with him.

Hirsch did not pay much attention to the suggestions—"We don't listen to cranks," he said—until Kleberg mentioned the idea of putting Ávila back up on Cañonero II.

"He advanced the theory, 'What have we got to lose?'" Hirsch said, referring to Kleberg. "Generally, it is a good idea to follow the boss' [sic] orders. He paid a million and a half for the colt, and I felt like he was more entitled to have something to say than anyone else."

In late August, Ávila accepted Hirsch's invitation to come to the United States and ride Cañonero II. When Ávila first got on Cañonero II, he found a horse that the rider thought had become frightened of the racetrack. It was that anxiety, Ávila surmised, that was causing Cañonero II's intractability. Hirsch's tack changes and Deas's gentle handling of the horse seemed to be working.

Cañonero II was the three-to-two favorite in the first start after being reunited with Ávila, an allowance race at one and one-sixteenth miles on September 20. It was the first time that Cañonero II had been favored since the Belmont Stakes the previous year. While there is no way to be certain, it is tempting to think that the New Yorkers who backed Cañonero II in the horse's failed quest for the Triple Crown were giving the horse and his Venezuelan jockey another chance, for old time's sake.

After leading for six furlongs, Cañonero II tired and dropped back to finish fifth. It was the first time since the Triple Crown that Cañonero II had shown the sort of early speed that had marked the horse's races in the Preakness Stakes and in the Belmont Stakes, and it was a harbinger of better things to come.

Cañonero II's next race, the one-and-one-eighth-mile Stymie Handicap, was one of the rare occasions—the first in seventeen years, since Swaps defeated Determine in the 1955 Californian Stakes—when two Kentucky Derby winners competed against each other.[147] Past performances won out over sentiment in the Stymie, and bettors made Meadow Stable's Riva Ridge, winner of the Kentucky Derby and Belmont Stakes earlier in the year, the odds-on choice. Cañonero II started at odds of nearly six to one.

The topweight under 123 pounds, 13 pounds more than Cañonero II carried, Riva Ridge set a blistering pace from the start, going a mile in 1:33⅖. After racing just off the pace through the early going, Cañonero II challenged Riva Ridge and the two horses matched each other stride for stride through the final eighth of a mile. Cañonero II drew away near the finish and won by five lengths, equaling the world record for one and one-eighth miles on dirt, 1:46⅕.

When Buddy Hirsch was inducted into racing's Hall of Fame at the National Museum of Racing in Saratoga Springs, New York, the plaque honoring the trainer said this about the Stymie:

> *Hirsch also nursed Cañonero II back to health after a series of setbacks in his 3-year-old season. Cañonero II ran his finest race when he defeated Hall of Famer Riva Ridge in the 1972 Stymie Handicap.*[148]

Cañonero II was supposed to meet Riva Ridge again in the Woodward Stakes ten days after the Stymie, where there would be a twenty-pound shift in weights. The Stymie winner would pick up sixteen pounds, and Riva Ridge would drop four pounds under the Woodward's weight-for-age conditions. Cañonero II was withdrawn from the Woodward after an ankle filled again, however, and the race was won by eventual three-year-old champion Key to the Mint.

Cañonero II had one more start with Ávila in the saddle, as the odds-on favorite in an allowance event over a muddy track at Aqueduct on October 20. The horse had the lead briefly but could not hold off the year's champion handicapper Autobiography and finished second. Cañonero II was supposed to make his last start in the Jockey Club Gold Cup a week later, but the horse was scratched on the morning of the race when the ankle swelling that had bothered him throughout the year returned. Autobiography won the Gold Cup by fifteen lengths, with Key to the Mint second and Riva Ridge third.

Although Cañonero II continued to race in the United States after being sold to King Ranch, he remained a superstar in Venezuela. An international television network planned a live broadcast of the Jockey Club Gold Cup to Venezuela and to islands in the Caribbean, but the ambitious plan was scrapped when Cañonero II was withdrawn from the race.

Cañonero II was retired with a record of nine victories from twenty-three starts and earnings of more than $360,000.[149]

A persistent question that arose during Cañonero II's Triple Crown campaign involved the training regimen laid out for the horse by Juan Arias. Did Cañonero II win because of Arias's unorthodox training—a mix of long, slow gallops with hardly any traditional speed work—or in spite of it? H.A. (Jimmy) Jones, who trained 1948 Triple Crown winner, Citation, at the time seemed to suggest that Arias's "unorthodox" style of training was appropriate only because Cañonero II was an "unorthodox" horse.[150] Years later, however, turf writer and handicapper Steve Davidowitz called Cañonero II's Derby win the "least-appreciated, most astounding upset of them all" and argued that Arias never received the widespread attention and acclaim he deserved as a trainer.[151]

The jury is still out, but two factors bear consideration: the frequency and the intensity of Cañonero II's workouts and the horse's physical condition.

During the weeks leading up to the Kentucky Derby, the Preakness Stakes and the Belmont Stakes, the number of workouts published by *Daily Racing Form* for Cañonero II was on par with most of the other three-year-olds on the Triple Crown trail in 1971. During Derby Week, for example, Arias worked Cañonero II once officially and once in secret. Bold Reason had two published works that week, while Jim French, Bold and Able and Bold Reason each had only one serious workout.

Cañonero II's works, with the exception of the unrecorded trip to the track early on the morning before the Derby, were excruciatingly slow, and critics argued that the horse was unprepared for his races as a result. Discounting the Belmont Stakes, when Cañonero II admittedly was short on training, the horse appeared to be as fit as he needed to be to win in the Derby and the Preakness. Even Buddy Hirsch learned that Cañonero II did not need frequent speed work to be at his best and that overtraining the horse was a risk. If there was second-guessing about the way Hirsch trained Cañonero II, it was ignored by the racing press.

Critics who said that Arias was not training like everyone else, which was true but not necessarily bad, sometimes overlooked the limitations on training imposed by Cañonero II's physical condition during the Triple Crown. The horse experienced a litany of problems before the Derby, before the Preakness and again before the Belmont Stakes, and his training schedule often was dictated by what he could do on any given day and not what Arias might have preferred.

The recurring thrush and the attempts to treat the problem were good examples. One of the reasons Arias ordered a new set of racing plates for Cañonero II prior to the Belmont Stakes was to allow a farrier to cut away the infected portion of the colt's frog so medication for the thrush could be applied to the hoof. Neither Arias nor the farrier shared a common language, however, and the farrier work did not go well. Cañonero II was sore and missed at least two days of work, at a point in the preparation for the Belmont when the horse could least afford it.

Problems with the shoeing job might have seemed inconsequential at the time, and that is how they were portrayed to the press and to the public prior to the race. Years later, however, Arias remains convinced that Cañonero II lost the bid for the Triple Crown the morning the horse was reshod. The farrier could not properly follow Arias's instructions, the trainer believes, because the two men could not communicate with each other.[152] Considering that any number of interpreters should have been available, proceeding without one was an inexcusable error during what might have been the most important moment in Cañonero II's preparation for the Belmont Stakes.

Arias also had a lot of free time on his hands with only one horse to train. He occupied himself by attending to Cañonero II, grazing the horse, petting his head, stroking his neck and talking to him. Nothing Arias did is peculiar behavior for a good horseman. What made Arias a lightning rod for criticism and the butt of jokes was his suggestion that his conversation with Cañonero II was a two-way street.

During a morning Breakfast-at-Belmont in late May, Arias explained to the assembled crowd that Cañonero II "told me six days before the Derby that he could win. At Pimlico, he told me on the Wednesday before the week of the race."

Someone asked Arias: "When will you know what Cañonero II tells you about the Belmont?"

The trainer laughed and replied: "Why? No one pays much attention to what I say."[153]

Whether Arias again fell victim to poor translations is impossible to know. Perhaps he meant that Cañonero II actually spoke to him or perhaps Arias simply meant that that he was being sensitive about cues to the horse's physical and mental state that helped guide the horse's training. The distinction did not matter to the reporters who began to portray Arias as some sort of black Dr. Dolittle—the man who talks to the animals in a series of children's books by author Hugh Lofting. It was a role that comedian Eddie Murphy would play for comic effect a quarter century later, but in 1971, the barbs hurled his way in print hurt Arias's credibility as a trainer and seriously wounded his pride.

It is no surprise, then, that over the years Arias has come to deny that he ever told reporters that he "talked" to Cañonero II. That may be understandable, but it is unfortunate. Whatever the basis, Juan Arias had a special connection to Cañonero II that played an important role in the horse's quest for the Triple Crown.

Chapter 7
ALL HEART

Although Cañonero II won the "one big race" in New York that both Robert J. Kleberg Jr. and Arthur B. Hancock Jr. wanted for the horse—his Stymie win over Riva Ridge in world-record time—he did not stand at Claiborne Farm as expected. Instead, the horse was syndicated by John R. Gaines and entered stud in 1973 at Gainesway Farm near Lexington, Kentucky. Cañonero II joined a blue-ribbon stallion roster at Gainesway, among them Horse of the Year Personality, Horse of the Year Vaguely Noble and juvenile champion Silent Screen. Kleberg died in October 1974, when Cañonero II's first foals were weanlings. The master of King Ranch did not live to see that he was only partially correct in his assessment of the horse. Like Pretendre, Cañonero II proved to be a better runner than he was a sire.

Blood-Horse magazine characterized the 1970s as "true golden years of racing and stallion making."[154] On the track, Cañonero II ushered in a decade of Triple Crown winners, near misses and spectacular racing with the victories in the Kentucky Derby and Preakness Stakes. As a sire, however, the horse was a disappointment.

Cañonero II received stacks of fan mail after retirement to Gainesway, but the horse never attracted much attention from mare owners and never sired a runner that even approached Cañonero's class and ability as a racehorse. From eight crops, Cañonero II sired 120 registered foals, an average of just 15 foals a year, including 5 stakes winners and 5 stakes-placed horses. Of those, the oddly named Cannon Boy, a filly, was the best. The filly

Cañonero II at Gainesway Farm. *Courtesy of Keeneland/*Thoroughbred Times.

won a division of the Chrysanthemum Handicap (gr. III) on turf and a division of the Athena Handicap on dirt and placed in the Pucker Up Stakes (gr. III), a division of the Boiling Springs Stakes (gr. III) and the Palomar Handicap (gr, III). Cannon Boy won nine of forty-four races and earned $188,702.

The sire's other stakes winners were Texas Gem (1980 Airline Stakes), Canon Law (a division of the 1980 Madison County Stakes and the 1981 Jet Diamond Stakes), Cocoroyale (a division of the 1981 Rambling Rose Handicap) and Papa Lynch (a division of the 1982 Mississippi Futurity). Other stakes-placed runners were Beach Boy, Gladiadora and Cappy's Dotti in the United States; El Tejano in Venezuela; and Rebellion in Belgium.

After several indifferent years standing at Gainesway Farm, Cañonero II was sold to a group of Venezuelans and exported to that country early in 1981. The horse died later in the year, on November 11, at the relatively young age of thirteen.

The cause of Cañonero II's death was reported in the media as a heart attack, but Juan Arias has a different, more sinister, theory. Arias suspects that Cañonero II was poisoned, the untimely demise the result of a disappointing record as a sire and a six-figure mortality insurance policy. There is no hard

"There was never anything wrong with Cañonero's heart." *Courtesy of the* Blood-Horse.

evidence that Cañonero II was killed because of a conspiracy, a grudge against someone associated with the horse, an extortion attempt or anything else other than a heart attack. In the end, it is better to remember Cañonero II as *Daily Racing Form* columnist Joe Hirsch did when he learned of the horse's death:

> *On Monday he was found dead in his stall. Through all his life, nothing came easy for him. He was tested to the limit, time and again. He didn't pass every test, but his courage was never at fault when he missed.*
>
> *The wire service from Caracas said that he died of a heart attack. That couldn't have been correct. There was never anything wrong with Cañonero's heart.* [155]

EPILOGUE

Attendance records were set in each of Cañonero II's Triple Crown races. The Derby and Preakness Stakes marks were short-lived, both falling the next year in Riva Ridge's Derby and in longshot Bee Bee Bee's Preakness Stakes. The Belmont Stakes attendance record, 82,694 fans, had more staying power, lasting twenty-eight years, until 1999. That year, as in 1971, there was a Triple Crown on the line in the Belmont Stakes. Charismatic, like Cañonero II, won the Derby as a longshot, gained credibility in the Preakness and started in the Belmont as the favorite. Charismatic had the lead in the stretch but eventually finished third behind winner Lemon Drop Kid. Jockey Chris Antley pulled Charismatic up after the finish, and it was discovered that the horse had suffered cannon bone and sesamoid fractures during the race. Charismatic survived the injuries and was exported to Japan for stud duty.

———•———

Pedro Baptista Sr. resolved his financial problems and continued to race Thoroughbreds in Venezuela until his death in 1984. Pedro Baptista Jr., who represented the Baptista family at Churchill Downs for Cañonero II's Kentucky Derby, is a successful businessman in Florida. He has no involvement in Thoroughbred racing.

The younger Baptista's memories of the 1971 Triple Crown are bittersweet. He recalls the Kentucky Derby as an "extraordinary and

Pedro Baptista Sr. (left) and Pedro Baptista Jr. accepted Cañonero II's Eclipse Award as champion three-year-old colt of 1971. *Courtesy of the Baptista Family and Salomon Gill.*

beautiful experience," but he also remembers the poor treatment Juan Arias received from the media and from much of the racing establishment. Even after the horse's spectacular win in Maryland, Baptista said, grudging compliments were qualified with comments about Cañonero II's "luck" and the mediocre quality of the field.

Baptista called Cañonero II's record-setting win two weeks later in the Preakness Stakes the "most beautiful race that I have ever seen in my life." Following the Preakness, "everybody's attitude changed about who Cañonero II was and if he had what it takes to be the winner or not of the Triple Crown." By the Belmont Stakes, "Venezuela was in a continual celebration. The entire U.S. was involved, and the media was covering Cañonero II and the story about the adventure."

Mostly, though, Baptista remembers his late father's dream and the "positive and triumphant attitude" Don Pedro had throughout Cañonero II's Triple Crown campaign.[156]

Juan Arias never matched the success he achieved with Cañonero II. He had a handful of job offers after he parted company with Pedro Baptista Sr. following the Belmont Stakes, but his efforts to establish himself as a trainer in the United States failed. The problem, he speculated, was that people expected too much from him. Speaking with *Daily Racing Form* columnist Teddy Cox at Laurel Race Course in Maryland, where he was training a few horses late in 1971, Arias said that "this is a tough way to go. Everyone expects me to come up with another Cañonero II tomorrow. It is not quite that easy, as you know. If you're lucky you get another like him in a lifetime."[157] After several lean years as a trainer back in his home country of Venezuela, Arias quit in favor of a government job in Caracas. He never strayed far from the racetrack, however, and after a stint as a steward at La Rinconada, he started training again.

Cañonero II at Pimlico Race Course. *Courtesy Keeneland/*Thoroughbred Times.

Arias did not fully grasp the significance of what he had accomplished with Cañonero II at the time and would not for years. Looking back at those magical weeks with Cañonero II, though, Arias has fond memories of the Triple Crown and of the horse that changed his life. He was heartbroken when Cañonero II died.

Cañonero II's legacy for everyone, Arias said, is "do not fear anything."

Gustavo Ávila and Cañonero II after crossing the finish line first in the 1971 Kentucky Derby. *Winants Brothers photo. Courtesy of* Blood-Horse.

Gustavo Ávila continued riding successfully, mostly in Venezuela and occasionally in the United States, until his retirement in the mid-1980s. He also worked as a steward at La Rinconada.

Although Team Cañonero was disbanded with the sale of the Derby and Preakness winner to King Ranch, Juan Arias and Gustavo Ávila both were back at Churchill Downs for the 1972 Kentucky Derby. Arias saddled eleventh-place finisher Hassi's Image; Ávila rode Pacallo, which ran last in the sixteen-horse field.

Juan Quintero, the groom who accompanied Cañonero II from Venezuela and who cared for the horse throughout his Triple Crown campaign,

Cañonero II's groom Juan Quintero tipped his hat to the crowd. *Courtesy Keeneland/* Thoroughbred Times.

became homeless after his return to Venezuela and has vanished from sight. Efforts to locate him, or even to determine if he still is alive, have been unsuccessful.

———•———

Horse racing and baseball traditionally have vied with each other for recognition as the most popular sport in Venezuela. Baseball has come out on top in recent years, due in large part to the scores of Venezuelan players who have come to the United States for successful major-league careers. The *Baseball Almanac* lists more than three hundred major-league players born in Venezuela, including Hall of Fame shortstop Luis Aparicio, Miguel Cabrera (the sport's first Triple Crown winner in forty-five years), two-time Cy Young Award winner Johan Santana, Omar Vizquel (who has the best all-time fielding percentage among shortstops), nine-time All Star Dave Concepción and on and on.[158]

Cañonero II's victories in the Kentucky Derby and Preakness Stakes, coupled with the horse's astonishing popularity in the United States, thrust Venezuelan racing into international prominence. The country now is a regional powerhouse, with Venezuelan-breds accounting for twelve wins in the Clásico del Caribe, the premier international race for horses from Caribbean-basin countries. Only Panama has been represented by more Clásico del Caribe winners, with thirteen as of this writing.

———•———

Racing continues at La Rinconada on the outskirts of Caracas most weekends, but over the years, the track has lost much of its glamour. It was one of South America's most beautiful facilities when it opened in 1959 with a backdrop of low mountains that evoked memories of Santa Anita in California. The spectacular mountains are still there, but the track itself now projects an air of quiet desperation. The elite still watch races from the luxury boxes where liquor flows and the air conditioning continues to function, but in other parts of the track, the seats are broken, the plumbing in the restrooms seldom works, the state-of-the-art veterinary hospital is in disrepair and entire families have taken up residence in the ramshackle grandstand. Although much of the betting has shifted off-track in recent years, the mere fact that La Rinconada continues to operate at all is testament to the enduring love Venezuelans have for horse racing.[159]

Although Jim French did not win the Kentucky Derby, the Preakness Stakes or the Belmont Stakes, the horse was the most consistent Triple Crown performer in 1971, the only horse placing in all three of the races (two second-place finishes and a third). Jim French was weighted among the best three-year-olds of 1971 on the Blood-Horse Free Handicap, below only Cañonero II (129 pounds), grass champion Run the Gantlet (128), Bold Reason (126) and Tinajero (125). Jim French and Bold Reasoning were assigned 124 pounds each.[160]

Jim French's performances on the track in 1971 were overshadowed by questions about who actually owned the colt. Bred by Ralph Wilson, longtime owner of the National Football League's Buffalo Bills, Jim French reportedly was sold to Long Island furniture dealer Frank J. Caldwell as a juvenile. Jim French raced in Caldwell's colors during the 1971 Triple Crown, but questions arose about hidden owners later in the year. After an investigation into the ownership of Jim French and other horses supposedly owned by Caldwell, the New York Racing Commission determined that the real owner of the horses was Robert LiButti, who was doing business under the name of Robert Presti. LiButti (or Presti), the commission said, had been ruled off the track during the late 1960s. Campo, Wilson and trainer George Poole were handed thirty-day suspensions for their roles in the concealed ownership.[161]

"We've got a real can of worms on our hands," New York steward Francis Dunne said of the ownership mess.

Jim French was retired during the summer of 1971 and sold for a reported $1 million to art dealer Daniel Wildenstein. The horse stood at stud in France, where he sired a handful of stakes winners, and then wound up in Japan.

The name of Dr. Mark Gerard shows up from time to time in a discussion of the 1971 Triple Crown, first as a member of the medical team that saved the life of Hoist the Flag and later as the treating veterinarian for Cañonero II after the colt was purchased by King Ranch. Dr. Gerard's career as a respected equine veterinarian came crashing down a few years later when he was implicated in a bizarre ringer scandal at Belmont Park that involved the substitution of a good horse named Cinzano for a cheap claimer named Lebon. The ersatz Lebon won and paid $116 for a $2 ticket, and Dr. Gerard walked away with some $80,000 stuffed in a paper sack. Represented in court by prominent criminal defense attorney F. Lee Bailey, Dr. Gerard was convicted of a misdemeanor and served time in prison.[162]

Cañonero II already has been the subject of an award-winning documentary, and a feature-length motion picture about the horse is in the works. *The Ballad of Cañonero II*, which focused on the Belmont Stakes, was released in 1972 and was a film festival award winner. Written by Stephen Glantz, who also wrote the music and theme song, *The Ballad of Cañonero II* was one of the first films to utilize multiple cameras to record a sporting event. The documentary's visual style influenced the coverage of horse racing and automobile sports for years.[163] *The Ballad of Cañonero II* is available online.

Viva Cañonero! is the working title for Salomon Gill's feature-length film, which is scheduled for release late in 2014. Gill was born in Venezuela.

The 1971 Kentucky Derby and Preakness Stakes winner was honored at Pimlico Race Course in 2012, when the Federico Tesio Stakes was renamed the Cañonero II Stakes. Juan Arias, Gustavo Avila and Pedro Baptista Jr. traveled to Maryland to present a trophy to the inaugural winner.

NOTES

Introduction

1. Gay, *Freud*, 104, quoting from Freud's seminal work *Interpretation of Dreams*. Additional information about Freud and his role in the development of dream interpretation and psychoanalysis can be found online at www.freud.org.uk, the official website of the Freud Museum in England.

2. Cañonero II got his name in Venezuela. Don Pedro enjoyed the sounds of "Cañoneros," bands of musicians who roamed the streets of Caracas, and he appropriated the name for his Pretendre colt. The "II" designation, indicating that a horse with the same name had been registered previously with the Jockey Club, was not appended to the name until the Kentucky-bred colt first was returned to the United States for racing. There will never be a Cañonero III. The Jockey Club's rules for naming horses, specifically Rule 6(F)(14)(c and g), prohibit the reuse of names of horses that won an Eclipse Award, a classic race (the Kentucky Derby, Preakness Stakes or Belmont Stakes) or a few other select events. The original Cañonero, a son of Grando de Oro—Tardy Helen, by Locust Bud—raced with little success for several years in the United States and in Mexico.

3. Edward L. Bowen, "The Hour of the Gunner," *Blood-Horse*, May 10, 1971, 1499.

4. William F. Reed, "What a Fiesta We Will Have," *Sports Illustrated*, May 31, 1971.

5. "I thought about buying Cañonero II as a two-year-old," Whittingham recalled. "They wanted either $80,000 or $60,000 for him. Nobody with him could speak English very well. That, and because I didn't get a firm figure, I forgot about it." *Daily Racing Form*, December 11, 1971. Whittingham was shopping for Mrs. Mary F. Jones, who raced grass champion Cougar II, a Chilean-bred, in 1972.

Chapter 1

6. Martin, "Miss Mananers."

7. http://www.kentuckyderby.com/road/schedule.

8. Challmas, *Preakness*, 204–9. The telephone call between Chick Lang and Don Pedro's representative has been told and retold, with some of the details evolving over time, until it has become an important part of the Cañonero II legend. Joseph J. Challmas interviewed Lang during the early 1970s for a Preakness Stakes history, and Lang's nearly contemporaneous account of the call likely is the most accurate version.

9. Venezuelan equine encephalitis is a mosquito-borne viral disease that can affect both horses and humans. Symptoms of the disease in humans include a flu-like syndrome accompanied by high fever and severe headaches. The disease can be fatal in both horses and humans. VEE first was identified as a separate disease following an outbreak in Venezuela in 1936 and first diagnosed in the United States in 1971. General information about VEE can be found in the *OIE Manual of Diagnostic Tests and Vaccines for Terrestrial Animals*, chap. 2.5.13, http://www.oie.int/fileadmin/Home/eng/Health_standards/tahm/2.05.13_VEE.pdf.

10. Joe Hirsch, "Impetuosity, Twist the Axe at Downs," *Daily Racing Form*, April 26, 1971.

11. Dean Eagle, "Well, Nobody Is Making Fun of Canonro II Now, Mr. Arias!" *Louisville Courier-Journal*, May 2, 1971.

12. Jim Bolus, "Bayonet Nearly Ended Jockey's Career," *Louisville Times*, May 29, 1973.

13. African American trainers were prominent during the last decades of the nineteenth century. Ansel "Andy" Williamson conditioned the first Derby winner, Aristides, in 1875; Edward D. Brown won in 1877 with Baden-Baden; William Bird won in 1884 with Buchanan; Alex Perry won in 1885 with Joe Cotton; and Dudley Allen won in 1891 with Kingman (a horse that he also owned). Williamson and Brown were voted into the Hall of Fame at the National Museum of Racing in Saratoga in 1984 and 1998, respectively. http://www.racingmuseum.org. Additional information about black trainers and jockeys in the Kentucky Derby can be found in Eclipse Award winning Wall, *How Kentucky Became Southern* and Saunders, *Black Winning Jockeys*.

14. Nicholson, *Kentucky Derby*, 153–58. Additional information about the racial climate in Louisville can be found in Garrow, *Bearing the Cross* and K'Meyer, *Civil Rights*.

15. In 1971, the cost for nominating a three-year-old to the Derby, Preakness and Belmont was $100 for each race, due when the nominations closed. For the Derby and Preakness, an owner paid an additional $1,000 to pass

the entry box, plus another $1,000 to actually have the horse start. For the Belmont, running a horse cost an owner $250 to enter and an additional $1,000 to start. The Belmont Stakes that year had one supplementary entry, for $5,000. During the next forty years, the cost of running a horse in the Derby far outraced inflation. The entry fee rose to $25,000, with an additional $25,000 required for a horse to start. Supplementary entries were allowed, for a whopping $200,000. The Preakness and Belmont Stakes both had entry and starting fees of $10,000, with supplemental entry fees set at $100,000. http://www.thetriplecrown.com.

16. *Blood-Horse*, January 11, 1971, 124. The Experimental Free Handicap was first published by the Jockey Club in 1935 as a vehicle for ranking the best two-year-olds of the year. Horses are weighted for a hypothetical race for two-year-olds at one and one-sixteenth miles on dirt. http://www.jockeyclub.com/exprimental.asp.

17. Kent Hollingsworth, "What's Going On Here," *Blood-Horse*, April 5, 1971.

18. "Cruguet to Get Back in the Saddle at Arlington," http://www.brisnet.com/cgi-bin/editorial/news/article.cgi?print=yes&id=23295.

19. Charles H. Stone, "Late News," *Blood-Horse*, March 29, 1971.

20. Joe Nichols, "Cañonero II, $19.40, Wins Derby," *New York Times*, May 2, 1971.

21. Smith and Anderson, *Red Smith Reader*, 78–79.

22. An excellent account of Hoist the Flag's groundbreaking surgeries and subsequent rehabilitation can be found in author Chew, "Dr. Jenny's Masterpiece," chap. 13 in *Kentucky Derby*.

23. William H. Rudy, "Hoist the Flag's Progress," *Blood-Horse*, May 24, 1971, 1658.

24. Hoist the Flag topped the 1970 Experimental at 126 pounds. Other high-weights were Limit to Reason (125); Executioner and Run the Gantlet (124); Peroudest Roman and Staunch Avenger (123); Ruffinal and Salem (122); Three Martinis (120); New Round, Pass Catcher and Raise Your Glass (119). The highest-weighted horse on the experimental to start in the Derby was Jim French (118). *Blood-Horse*, January 11, 1971, 124.

25. Dancer's Image, which finished first in the 1968 running, was the only Derby winner from 1965 through 1970 to be weighted on the Experimental Free Handicap, earning a 115-pound assessment. Dancer's Image was disqualified after a controversial medication test and years of legal wrangling. Forward Pass, assigned 114 pounds on the 1967 Experimental, was declared the winner.

26. Mike Barry, "Your Wait Is Over; Here Is Barry's Pick," *Louisville Courier-Journal*, May 1, 1971.

27. Dean Eagle, "97th Running Could Be Called 'Derby of Missing'," ibid.

28. Frank T. Phelps, "Cañonero II's Victory Nice But Alarming for Future Derby," *Lexington Leader*, May 3, 1971.

29. *Time*, "Sport: A Gunner Makes History," May 10, 1971.

Chapter 2

30. Often associated with Robert A. Heinlein's science-fiction classic, the phrase "stranger in a strange land" actually has biblical origins: "And she gave him a son, and he called his name Gershom; for he said, I have been a stranger in a strange land." Exodus 2:22.

31. Dave Kindred, "Before You Laugh, Remember—$1,200 Horse Has Last Laugh," *Louisville Courier-Journal*, May 2, 1971.

32. Chew, *Kentucky Derby*, 131.

33. Will Grimsley, "Lonely Monarch: While His Coterie Celebrates, Cañonero II Walks a Silent Mile," *Louisville Courier-Journal*, May 2, 1971.

34. Eagle, "Well, Nobody."

35. "Hollywood Park Architect Arthur Froehlich Is Dead," *Los Angeles Times*, October 5, 1985, http://articles.latimes.com/1985-10-05/sports/sp-1206_1_hollywood-park.

36. Ibid.

37. Reed, "What a Fiesta."

38. Edward L. Bowen, personal communication with the author, August 28, 2013.

39. Robert Hebert, "New Kentucky Derby Favorite," *Blood-Horse*, April 12, 1971, 1188.

40. Milton C. Tony, *Dancer's Image: The Forgotten Story of the 1968 Kentucky Derby* (Charleston, SC: The History Press, 2011) is my award-winning account of the controversial disqualification of Dancer's Image.

41. Jim Bolus, *Louisville Courier-Journal*, April 6, 1970.

42. Whitney Tower, "They're All Running After the Flag," *Sports Illustrated*, April 5, 1971.

43. Pat Harmon, "Cañonero Was a dream Horse," *Cincinnati Post*, undated clipping archived at the Kentucky Derby Museum, Louisville, Kentucky.

44. http://www.anecdotashipicas.net/Jinetes/Gustavo/Avila.php.

45. As of this writing, horses from Panama have won thirteen runnings of the Clásico, followed by Venezuela (twelve), Mexico (ten), Puerto Rico (eight), Colombia (one) and the Dominican Republic (one). Other countries represented in the annual race are Jamaica, Trinidad and Tobago, Ecuador, Costa Rica and Guatemala.

46. G.F.T. Ryall, The Race Track, *New Yorker*, January 31, 1959. Ryall wrote his *New Yorker* column under the pen name Audax Minor in honor of noted British racing writer Arthur Fitzhardinge Berkeley Portman, who signed his articles "Audax."

47. Ward Sinclair, "A Horse of the People," *Louisville Courier-Journal*, May 21, 1971.

48. Chew, *Kentucky Derby*, 131.

49. Joe Hirsch, "Derby Hero's Next Start in Preakness," *Daily Racing Form*, May 4, 1971.

50. Cliff Giulliams, "Jose Rodriquez' Bizarre Derby Win," *Louisville Courier-Journal*.

51. Jim Bolus, "Bayonet Nearly Ended Jockey's Career," *Louisville Times*, May 29, 1973. The early morning workout was first reported by Jim Bolus two years later, as three furlongs in 0:35. A subsequent report twenty years after the fact lowered the time to 0:34⅕.

52. Chew, *Kentucky Derby*, 131.

53. Whitney Tower, "Deep in the Heart of…," *Sports Illustrated*, June 12, 1972.

54. William H. Rudy, "Hoist the Flag's Progress," *Blood-Horse*, May 24, 1971.

55. Barney Nagler, "'Personal Vet' Denies Story of Cañonero II's Crooked Leg," *Daily Racing Form*, May 14, 1971.

56. Bob Adair, "$1,200 Colt Earns $145,500 for His Venezuelan Owner," *Louisville Courier-Journal*, May 2, 1971.

57. http://www.jocokeyclub.com/factbook/foalcrop-nabd,html.

58. Herb Goldstein, "Jockeys Agree, Simply Too Many Derby Starters," *Daily Racing Form*, May 3, 1971.

59. Bowen, "Hour of the Gunner."

60. Whitney Tower, "Missing Information Unavailable," *Sports Illustrated*, May 10, 1971.

61. Sinclair, "Horse of the People."

62. Hugh J. McGuire, "Combs Says Cañonero II's Win Good for Racing Everywhere," *Daily Racing Form*, May 13, 1971.

63. Cawood Ledford, "Coffee in the Morning, Roses in the Afternoon," *Blood-Horse*, April 18, 1992.

CHAPTER 3

64. George Rorrer, "No Giveaway," *Louisville Courier-Journal*, May 2, 1971.

65. Extensive information about Cañonero II's pedigree and Edward B. Benjamin's role as breeder of the Kentucky Derby winner can be found at Charles H. Stone, "Derby Winner's Pedigree" and Kent Hollingsworth, "A Pattern That Worked," *Blood-Horse*, May 10, 1971.

66. Hunter, *American Classic Pedigrees*, 388.

67. Chew, *Kentucky Derby*, 129.

68. Keeneland's select summer sale was discontinued in 2002 as a result of Mare Reproductive Loss Syndrome, a disease that decimated the Kentucky foal crop the previous spring. In its place is an expanded fall sale incorporating several "select" sessions along with the traditional nonselect fall sales offerings.

69. William S. Evans to Jim Bolus, October 24, 1979, archived at the Kentucky Derby Museum, Louisville, Kentucky.

70. Hollingsworth, "A Pattern."

71. *Blood-Horse*, "Demand Still Strong for Quality Stock," September 20, 1969.

72. Joe Hirsch, "Navas Launched Cañonero II Saga," *Daily Racing Form*, May 15, 1971.

73. Sinclair, "Horse of the People."

74. Bowen, "Hour of the Gunner."

75. Rorrer, "No Giveaway."

76. Frank Deford, ed., "They Said It," *Sports Illustrated*, May 17, 1971.

CHAPTER 4

77. Reed, "What a Fiesta."

78. Whitney Tower, "Arriba! Cañonero Does It Again," *Sports Illustrated*, May 24, 1971.

79. Barney Nagler, "Favorite or Not, Cañonero II Commanding Most Attention," *Daily Racing Form*, May 15, 1971.

80. Whitney Tower, "It May Be Adios to Cañonero," *Sports Illustrated*, May 17, 1971.

81. A good summary of the acclimatization effect can be found at the website of the Institute for Altitude Medicine: http://www.altitudemedicine.org/index.php/altitude-medicine/athletes-and-altitude.

82. Edward L. Bowen, "The Nonconformist," *Blood-Horse*, May 24, 1971.

83. Barney Nagler, "Cañonero II's 'Speed Test' Produces Laughs at Pimlico," *Daily Racing Form*, May 13, 1971.

84. Barney Nagler, "Favorite or Not, Cañonero II Commanding Most Attention," ibid., May 15, 1971.

85. "Cañonero II Has Slow Heart," *Lexington Leader*, May 11, 1971.

86. Joe Hirsch, "Pair Provide Formidable Test For Derby Hero Cañonero II," *Daily Racing Form*, May 15, 1971.

87. Tower, "Arriba!"

88. Joe Hirsch, "Cañonero II Wins Preakness," *Daily Racing Form*, May 17, 1971.

89. http://www.pimlico.com/race-info/track-records.

90. *Daily Racing Form*, "Venezuelans Jubilant on Cañonero II's Score," May 18, 1971.

91. Sinclair, "Horse of the People."

92. Uli Schmetzer, "Cañonero II New Hero in Venezuela," *Daily Racing Form*, May 19, 1971.

93. http://www.drf.com/news/top-10-preakness-stakes-moments.

94. More information about the dispute over Secretariat's time in the 1971 Preakness can be found at Victor Mather, "It's Secretariat, Faster Today Than in 1973," *New York Times*, June 21, 2012, and http://www.secretariat.com.

95. Penny Chenery, interview by Jayne Miller, WBAL-TV, June 20, 2012, http://www.wbaltv.com/news/maryland/Maryland-Racing-Commission-rules-in-Secretariat-s-favor/-/9379376/15161130/-/sejp7fz/-/index.html.

96. Hirsch, "Cañonero II."

97. Ibid.

98. Bowen, "Nonconformist."

99. Sinclair, "Horse of the People."

100. Joe Hirsch, "Next Stop Belmont for Cañonero II," *Daily Racing Form*, May 18, 1971.

101. Reed, "What a Fiesta."

Chapter 5

102. Attributed to New York Yankees star Yogi Berra, who was awed by watching Mickey Mantle and Roget Maris hit back-to-back home runs on numerous occasions. http://www.baseballnation.com/2012/6/23/3112502/bryce-harper-clown-question-bro-baseball-quotations.

103. This quirk in scheduling occurred on eleven occasions prior to 1931, when the Derby-Preakness-Belmont order of go was firmly established. In two years, 1917 and 1922, the Derby and Preakness were run on the same day. http://turfnsport.com/preakness-stakes/.

104. *New York Times*, "Horses from East Arrive for Derby," May 15, 1923.

105. Bennett Liebman, "Origins of the Triple Crown," The Rail, *New York Times*, April 24, 2008.

106. Chew, *Kentucky Derby*, 145.

107. Toby, *Dancer's Image*.

108. Whitney Tower, "The Man Takes Charge of His Horse," *Sports Illustrated*, June 2, 1969.

109. Whitney Tower, "The Prince Ducks the Big One," ibid., May 26, 1969.

110. "Cañonero II Gallops Once around Belmont," *Daily Racing Form*, May 22, 1971.

111. Herb Goldstein, "Vets Report Skin Rash Not Serious," ibid., May 28, 1971.

112. Teddy Cox, "Laurel Race Course…," ibid., December 23, 1971.

113. Goldstein, "Vets Report."

114. "Thwarting Thrush," http://www.thehorse.com/articles/20341/thwarting-thrush.

115. Herb Goldstein, "Claim Ailing Cañonero II Will Run," *Daily Racing Form*, May 31, 1971.

116. Ibid.

117. Edward L. Bowen, "Decline and Fall of a Superstar," *Blood-Horse*, June 16, 1971.

118. Charles Hatton, "Cañonero II Rumors Obscure Today's Mother Goose Stakes," *Daily Racing Form*, May 29, 1971.

119. Goldstein, "Claim Ailing Cañonero II Will Run."

120. Herb Goldstein, "Cañonero II Has Long Gallops on Grass under Strong Hold," *Daily Racing Form*, June 1, 1971.

121. Ibid.

122. Bob Horwood, "No Sale of Cañonero II Before Belmont Stakes," *Daily Racing Form*, May 22, 1971.

123. Teddy Cox, "Rivals 'Watch Out for' Cañonero II," ibid., June 5, 1971.

124. Whitney Tower, "The Happy Story Ends," *Sports Illustrated*, June 14, 1971.

125. Scorecard, *Sports Illustrated*, June 7, 1971. A week later, on June 14, 1971, the cover of the magazine showed an image of Pass Catcher winning the Belmont Stakes and carried this headline: "Cañonero Should Not Have Run."

126. Herb Goldstein, "Monmouth Invitational Next 'Big' Race for Pass Catcher," *Daily Racing Form*, June 8, 1971.

127. Walter Blum's recollections of the 1971 Belmont Stakes were taken from an interview with the jockey conducted by filmmaker Salomon Gill.

128. Ibid.

129. Herb Goldstein, "Belmont Notes," *Daily Racing Form*, June 8, 1971.

130. Teddy Cox, "Pass Catcher Wins Belmont," ibid., June 7, 1971.

131. Goldstein, "Belmont Notes."

132. Herb Goldstein, "Report Sale of Cañonero II Near," *Daily Racing Form*, June 10, 1971.

133. Scorecard, "Black Day in Caracas," *Sports Illustrated*, June 14, 1971.

Chapter 6

134. G.F.T. Ryall, The Race Track, *New Yorker*, June 19, 1971.

135. For an excellent account of Robert J. Kleberg's career as a breeder and owner of Thoroughbreds, see Bowen, *Legacies*, 33–48.

136. Tower, "Deep in the Heart."

137. William H. Rudy, "Cañonero II May Come Back," *Daily Racing Form*, September 6, 1971.

138. Herb Goldstein, "Cañonero II Improving; Future Plans Indefinite," ibid., June 17, 1971.

139. Rudy, "Cañonero II May Come Back."

140. Cañonero II also was assigned top weight of 129 pounds on the Bood-Horse Free Handicap for three-year-olds of 1971. Stud News, "Cañonero II Retired," *Blood-Horse*, November 6, 1972

141. "A Crusher for Arias: Cañonero Sale Would Hurt," *Palm Beach Post*, May 19, 1971.

142. William H. Rudy, "Once More, The Thunder," *Blood-Horse*, October 2, 1972.

143. William J. Hirsch detailed the trials and tribulations of training Cañonero II for *Daily Racing Form* (Teddy Cox, "Cañonero's Remarkable Return Made Through Trial and Error," September 27, 1972) and *Blood-Horse* magazine (Rudy, "Once More, The Thunder").

144. Kent Hollingsworth, "What's Going On Here," *Blood-Horse*, August 21, 1972.

145. Tower, "Deep in the Heart."

146. Ibid.

147. Rarer still is a race in which two Triple Crown winners meet. That has only happened twice, in the 1978 Marlboro Cup and in the same year's Jockey Club Gold Cup. Seattle Slew, winner of the Triple Crown in 1977, defeated 1978 Triple Crown winner Affirmed by three lengths in the Marlboro Cup. The two Triple Crown winners met again in the Jockey Club Gold Cup, where both were defeated by Exceller. The only other horse to defeat two Triple Crown winners, albeit in different races, was Charles S. Howard's Noor. Irish-bred Noor defeated 1948 Triple Crown winner Citation on four occasions in 1950—in the Santa Anita, San Juan Capistrano, Forty-Niners and Golden Gate Handicaps—and beat 1946 Triple Crown winner Assault in the 1950 Hollywood Gold Cup. The career of Noor is the subject of the my award-winning *Noor: A Champion Thoroughbred's Unlikely Journey from California to Kentucky* (Charleston, SC: The History Press, 2012); Hudson, *Horse Racing's Most Wanted*, 43.

148. http://www.racingmuseum.org/hall-of-fame/horse-trainers-view.asp?varID=21.

149. There are minor discrepancies in Cañonero II's career earnings, likely due to fluctuating currency conversions. *Daily Racing Form* listed the earnings as $361,006 (Daily Racing Form, *Champions*, 258); the *Blood-Horse* listed the earnings as $360,980 (Stud News, "Cañonero II Retired," November 6, 1972); and they were listed as $360,933 at www.equineline.com.

150. Whitney Tower, "The Happy Story Ends," *Sports Illustrated*, June 14, 1971.

151. Davidowitz, *Best and Worst*, 18–26.

152. Interview with Juan Arias conducted by Salomon Gill.

153. Herb Goldstein, "Conditioner Again Puts Down Rumors" *Daily Racing Form*, May 29, 1971.

Chapter 7

154. Anne Peters, Breeding, "Kentucky Derby Winners as Sires," *Blood-Horse*, May 18, 2013.

155. Joe Hirsch, "Nothing Came Easy," *Daily Racing Form*, November 13, 1981.

EPILOGUE

156. Pedro Baptista Jr., interview with Salomon Gill.

157. Teddy Cox, "Laurel Race Course…," ibid., December 23, 1971.

158. http://www.baseball-almanac.com/players/birthplace.php?loc=Venezuela.

159. Christopher Toothaker, "Horse Racing a Strong 2nd to Baseball in Venezuela," http://usatoday30.usatoday.com/sports/horses/2010-12-10-995780388_x.htm.

160. *Blood-Horse*, January 17, 1972.

161. Whitney Tower, "A Thoroughbred Can of Worms," *Sports Illustrated*, August 30, 1971; Steve Haskin, "The Strange Saga of Jim French," http://cs.bloodhorse.com/blogs/horse-racing-steve-haskin/archive/2011/03/20/hangin-with-haskin-the-strange-saga-of-jim-french.aspx.

162. http://www.bloodhorse.com/horse-racing/articles/63776/mark-j-gerard-substituted-ringer-dies.

163. http://www.zoominfo.com/p/Stephen-Glantz/1607024893.

BIBLIOGRAPHY

Beltran, David Jiménez. *Agua Caliente: Remembering Mexico's Legendary Racetrack*. Lexington, KY: Eclipse Press, 2004.

Blood-Horse.

Blood-Horse. *Greatest Kentucky Derby Upsets*. Lexington, KY: Eclipse Press 2007.

———. *Horse Racing's Top 100 Moments*. Lexington, KY: Eclipse Press, 2008.

———. *10 Best Kentucky Derbies*. Lexington, KY: Eclipse Press, 2005.

———. *Thoroughbred Champions: Top 100 Racehorses of the 20th Century*. Lexington, KY: Blood-Horse Publications, 1999.

Bowen, Edward L. *Legacies of the Turf: A Century of Great Thoroughbred Breeders*. Vol. 2. Lexington, KY: Eclipse Press, 2004.

Challmas, Joseph J. *The Preakness: A History*. Severna Park, MD: 1975.

Chew, Peter. *The Kentucky Derby: The First 100 Years*. Boston: Houghton Mifflin Co., 1974.

Cincinnati Post.

Daily Racing Form.

Daily Racing Form. *Champions: The Lives, Times, and Past Performances of America's Greatest Thoroughbreds*. Rev. ed. *Champions from 1893–2004*. New York: Daily Racing Form Press, 2005.

Davidowitz, Steve. *The Best and the Worst of Thoroughbred Racing*. New York: Daily Racing Form Press, 2007.

Freud, Sigmund. *The Interpretation of Dreams*. New York, London: W.W. Norton & Co., 2006.

Garrow, David J. *Bearing the Cross: Martin Luther King Jr. and the Southern Christian Leadership Conference*, New York: W. Morrow, 1986.

Gay, Peter. *Freud: A Life for Our Time*. New York: W.W. Norton & Co., 2006.

Hewitt, Abram S. *Sire Lines*. Updated ed. Lexington, KY: Eclipse Press, 2006.

Hudson, David L., Jr. *Horse Racing's Most Wanted: The Top 10 Book of Derby Delights, Frenetic Finishes, and Backstretch Banter*. Dulles, VA: Potomac Books, 2011.

Hunter, Avalyn. *American Classic Pedigrees*. Lexington KY: Eclipse Press, 2003.

K'Meyer, Tracy E. *Civil Rights in the Gateway to the South*. Lexington: University Press of Kentucky, 2009.

Los Angeles Times.

Louisville Courier-Journal.

Louisville Times.

Martin, Judith. "Miss Manners: On Dealing with Unannounced Visitors," http://living.msn.com/love-relationships/article?cp-documentid=30937848.

New Yorker.

New York Times.

Nicholson, James C. *The Kentucky Derby: How the Run for the Roses Became America's Premier Sporting Event*. Lexington: University Press of Kentucky, 2012.

Palm Beach Post.

Saunders, James Robert. *Black Winning Jockeys in the Kentucky Derby*. Jefferson, NC: McFarland & Co., 2003.

Smith, Red, and Dave Anderson, eds. *The Red Smith Reader*. New York: Vintage Books, 1983.

Sowers, Richard. *The Abstract Primer of Thoroughbred Racing: Separating Myth From Fact to Identify the Genuine Gems & Dandies 1946–2003*. Stockbridge, GA: Old Sport Publishing Co., 2004.

Sports Illustrated.

Time.

Wall, Maryjean. *How Kentucky Became Southern: A Tale of Outlaws, Horse Thieves, Gamblers, and Breeders*. Lexington: University Press of Kentucky, 2010.

ABOUT THE AUTHOR

Milt Toby has been writing about Thoroughbred racing for more than forty years. His seven previous books include two national award winners published by The History Press: *Dancer's Image: The Forgotten Story of the 1968 Kentucky Derby* (winner of the Dr. Tony Ryan Book Award as the best book about Thoroughbred racing released in 2011 and an American Horse Publications editorial award as the best horse book of that year) and *Noor: A Champion Thoroughbred's Unlikely Journey from California to Kentucky* (winner of an American Horse Publications editorial award as the best horse book of 2012). Milt lives in Central Kentucky with his wife, Roberta, plus a Dalmatian, a Doberman and two rescue cats. Visit his website at www.miltonctoby.com.

CPSIA information can be obtained
at www.ICGtesting.com
Printed in the USA
BVHW04*1437300718
523024BV00012B/284/P